Series / Number 02-014

A General Empirical Typology
of Foreign Policy Behavior

CHARLES W. KEGLEY, Jr.
University of South Carolina

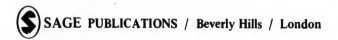 **SAGE PUBLICATIONS** / Beverly Hills / London

For information address:

SAGE PUBLICATIONS, INC.
275 South Beverly Drive
Beverly Hills, California 90212

SAGE PUBLICATIONS, INC.
St George's House / 44 Hatton Garden
London EC1N 8ER

International Standard Book Number 0-8039-0250-6

Library of Congress Catalog Card No. L.C. 73-79386

FIRST PRINTING

When citing a professional paper, please use the proper form. Remember to cite the
correct Sage Professional Paper series title and include the paper number. One of the
two following formats can be adapted (depending on the style manual used):

(1) CAPORASO, J. A. (1972) Functionalism and Regional Integration: A Logical
    and Empirical Assessment. Sage Professional Paper in International Studies
    02-004. Beverly Hills and London: Sage Pubns.

OR

(2) Caporaso, James A., *Functionalism and Regional Integration: A Logical and
    Empirical Assessment.* Beverly Hills and London: Sage Professional Paper in
    International Studies 02-004, 1972.

CONTENTS

A General Empirical Typology
of Foreign Policy Behavior

CHARLES W. KEGLEY, Jr.
University of South Carolina

INTRODUCTION

Although the research orientation known as "the comparative study of foreign policy" is still in its infancy, considerable consensual disappointment exists in the amount of progress the movement has been able to realize thus far. Every field of inquiry seems to undergo birth pains in its first feeble attempts to break out of what Kuhn (1962) has termed the "prescientific" phase of investigation, but for the scientific study of foreign policy the embarkation has been particularly agonizing. One of the most conspicuous sources of failure—if one uses the frequency that the problem is noted in the literature as his yardstick—seems to be that students of the field have been negligent in confronting the problem of measurement of their basic variables. While we have been fairly successful in isolating the various factors relevant to foreign policy and have even managed to devise some compelling hypotheses and models of the nexus between them, we have been remiss in undertaking systematic measure-

AUTHOR'S NOTE: *This is a revision of a paper presented at the Annual Convention of the International Studies Association, Dallas, Texas, March 17, 1972. For their thoughtful comments and criticism on this paper, I feel especially indebted to Patrick J. McGowan, William D. Coplin, Michael K. O'Leary, Philip M. Burgess, Fred A. Sondermann, Joseph M. Scolnick, James A. Kuhlman, William O. Chittick, Stephen L. Mills, Gary D. Hoggard, Robert M. Rood, and Richard A. Skinner. None of these, of course, should be burdened with any responsibility for the weaknesses of the present text.*

ment of the policy behavior of nations. Indeed, measurement is the sine qua non of scientific research, without which progress in the acquisition of knowledge is precluded. As Torgerson (1958: 2) has argued: "The development of a theoretical science . . . would seem to be virtually impossible unless its variables can be measured adequately."

Many contend that for any emerging field, a good place to begin is with the formation of classificatory schemes. Typology construction is considered to be the most appropriate first requisite in the scientific study of any phenomena, and is often conceived as a form of measurement itself (McGowan, 1970: 3). As Kalleberg (1966: 3) has observed,

> Science must first of all discriminate. This is the ultimate ground of all scientific measurement, from the simplest procedures of empirical classification based on observation, to comparison, and finally to the complex constructions of quantitative theory.

And Sjoberg (1970: 38) has suggested that for progress in the scientific search for generalizations to proceed, a good starting point would be the construction of typological categories:

> perhaps the major emphasis should be given to developing more satisfactory invariant reference points or universal categories. In order to test . . . relationships . . . certain comparable and relatively stable categories must be employed.

If we can accept the contention that in the broadest sense the most basic problem confronting foreign policy analysis is the measurement one, it seems equally arguable that the portion of international conduct most in need of typological differentiation and measurement is the principal (McClelland, 1970: 4) dependent variable of foreign policy analysis: "foreign policy output" or the external behavior of states. Again, a reading of the literature reveals wide agreement that measurement of the foreign actions of states, what nations do abroad, has been largely ignored and received minimal systematic treatment. Thus we find Puchala (1969a: 2) complaining that

> We have not as yet devised any very productive quantitative indices of foreign policy output. In effect, correlations between input and output have eluded us, because we have not been able to systematically define, analyze, operationalize, and chart foreign policy.

Similarly, we hear Burgess (1970: 5) suggesting that

A primary task for political science is the examination of policy outcomes. . . . Empirically useful ways of thinking about national actions and for conceptualizing and measuring policy outcomes are urgently needed.

Given this consensus on the research priorities for foreign policy analysis, this research will limit its focus and aim to develop an empirically based typology of only the external behavior of nations, so as to distinguish the various types of foreign action. This decision reflects a judgment on the part of the investigator that the measurement of inputs, those independent variables which predict external performance, is currently receiving adequate attention (Young, 1970: 4). It is believed that the suspected causes of state behavior, such as national attributes and systemic pattern variables, have thus far obtained most of the treatment, and that there is validity to Young's (1970: 4) assessment that

Unfortunately, very few have even considered the desirability of grouping nations on the basis of some aspect of their external behavior rather than according only to non-behavioral descriptors of nations such as political system, level of development, etc.

Thus the rationale for a limited focus stems from the belief that not until we can build a typology of the categories of external action will we be able to get on with the generation and testing of foreign policy theory which links these output types with existing measures of foreign policy determinants. That is, in order to discover which domestic processes or variations in systemic structures are associated with which types of foreign policy outputs, a classification system for foreign policy output is needed; McClelland (1970: 20-21) notes with displeasure that "virtually no work on this taxonomy has been undertaken to date." Our ability to get on with the advancement of systematic foreign policy theory is contingent upon the completion of this prior task.

KINDS OF FOREIGN POLICY TYPOLOGIES

Because all description and explanation are contingent upon some sort of previous conceptualization (Meehan, 1968: 36; Hempel, 1952)[1], a variety of typologies have of necessity been devised for the purpose of analyzing foreign policy output behavior. Three kinds of such foreign policy typologies currently in use in the literature may be distinguished. The first and most frequent may be termed *definitional* ones; the second may be called *ad hoc* typologies; and thirdly, there exist *empirical* typologies.

Since there exist many logically distinct forms of theory, it should be emphasized that this paper is concerned solely with the construction of *general positive theory* (McGowan, 1971) and that consequently the discussion which follows will only assess the contribution which each type of typology makes in the generation of such theories. This focus stems from the author's conviction that general positive theory (theories at a high level of generality which are amenable to empirical refutation) is the type of theory construction most in need of treatment in the field of foreign policy studies. We will thus be operating from the scientific paradigm which views nomothetic generalization as the most rewarding goal of social inquiry.

(A) Definitional typologies. Definitional typifications are devised according to the observer's mental model of the distinguishing features of state behavior. The categorization rests on the assumption that the classes defined represent characteristics which cluster empirically. Cicourel (1964: 21-22) described the process by which such conceptualizations by postulation are typically formulated:

> Our lack of methodological sophistication means that the decision procedures for categorizing social phenomena are buried in implicit common-sense assumptions about the actor . . . and the observer's own views about everyday life. The procedures seem intuitively "right" or "reasonable" . . . the coupling between category and observation is often based upon what are considered to be "obvious" "rules" which any "intelligent" coder or observer can "easily" encode and decode.

The following table summarizes some of the more popular and conventional definitional classifications employed in the literature to describe and categorize the behavioral patterns of nations (see Table 1 below).[2]

The multidimensionality of external phenomena (Etzioni and Lehman, 1969: 49-50) suggests why so many competing definitions exist of the classes by which interstate behavior may be differentiated. Because individuals manifest different cognitive styles in categorizing objects (Gardner, 1953: 214-233; Mischel, 1968: 16-20), and because common-sense distinctions in phenomena are usually formed in terms of a few categorical differentiations in spite of cognizance of other differences (Stinchcombe, 1968: 41; Gardner, 1953: 230), complex phenomena like foreign policy may be expected to be typified in myriad ways. Such efforts attempt to define an operationally workable number of categories which group homogeneous forms of external action without obscuring important differences among these forms.

The limitations of definitional typologies include the following: (1) they are not amenable to validation; (2) they tend to be fraught with implicit normative assumptions and emotive connotations (Rosenau, 1969a: 149-171); (3) lacking operationalism specifying empirical referents, their classes fail to convey intersubjectively transmissible meaning; and (4) because they are derived from the everyday phraseology of practioners of statecraft, they invite semantic confusion (Sullivan, 1963: Madge, 1965: 25-31).

However, these deficiencies do not preclude definitional typologies from playing a useful role in positive theory construction. The utility of definitional typologies in theory construction lies in their ability to organize perceptions about the subject in some preliminary fashion so that some initial hypotheses can be generated and a base can be established for the eventual reformulation and refinement of conceptualizations; they are convenient constructs for suggesting possible classes into which the phenomena might fall. Thus definitional typologies are sometimes referred to as "heuristic" ones (Winch, 1947: 68-75). Abstract conceptualizations of the qualitative types of foreign policy heuristically suggest concepts with names for communicating about foreign policy, propose something of how foreign policy behavior might be treated, and direct our observations to the presumably most relevant features of external behavior. The types formed by definition thereby posit which aspects of foreign policy behavior are the most important and are subject to the most variation. Although these categories do not themselves comprise a theory (Argyle, 1957: 60-61; McGowan, 1972: 1), they facilitate theory formation by providing constructs which may be speculatively linked to form hypothetical or theoretical statements (nomethetic generalizations) which if eventually operationalized are amenable to empirical verification.

Hence, definitional typologies are not theories, but their formation constitutes a necessary first step in the construction of positive foreign policy theory. Definitional typification "is the way the scientist begins his scientific analysis" (Isaak, 1969: 72). Despite their inability to contribute to the testing of positive theory, definitional typologies help to conceptualize foreign behavior and therefore may be said to play an important role in theory construction. But they are not sufficient in themselves.

(B) Ad hoc typologies. A second kind of typology results when the researcher departs from the classifications of conventional verbal language and attempts to devise a set of categories for the systematic observation of foreign policy output behavior. Ad hoc typologies order the complexity of foreign policy output phenomena in an operationally useful manner, so that the domain of foreign policy behavior can be organized in a

TABLE 1
Types of Foreign Policy as Identified by Various Scholars

Dimension	Coplin[a]	Holsti[b]	Kulski[c]	Lerche & Said[d]	London[e]	Modelski[f]
Rank, Status, Involvement	great power (supra-regional)/ small power (regional)	domination/ dependence	superpowers/ great powers/ semideveloped countries/ underdeveloped states	great powers/ medium powers/ small powers		
Policy Toward Change	status quo/ revisionist	avoidance/ conquest/ submission/ withdrawal/ compromise/ awards/ passive	status quo/ revolutionary/ revisionist	satisfied (conserving)/ dissatisfied (change); status quo/ revisionist	traditional/ revolutionaly	defensive/ community building (offensive) objectives
Cold War Orientation	East/West/ neutral		communist powers/Western powers/ uncommitted third world	West/non-West	socialist/ Western/ noncommitted	
Economic Capability	rich/poor		developed/ underdeveloped	modern/under-developed		
Activity-Passivity	intervention-ist/nonin-tervenionist	coalition maker/non-alignment isolation	intervention	balancing objectives/ hegemonic objectives	balancing of power/isola-tion, autarky, neutralism	

TABLE 1 (Continued)

Dimension	Coplin[a]	Holsti[b]	Kulski[c]	Lerche & Said[d]	London[e]	Modelski[f]
Affect	hostility/ friendship	collaboration/ competition/ conflict	active defense/ passive defense/ offense	violent conflict/ nonviolent conflict; coercion/persuasion/adjustment/agreement	detente	
Normative-Motivational Aspect			national interests/ principled foreign policy	realistic/ ideological		principled "interests" or "objectives"
Form/ Substance	perceived/ actual		policies of power/policies of prestige	prestige and image/coercive influence		
Hierarchy of Goal Preference	definition of the situation/ goal selection/ search for alternatives/ choosing alternatives	core interests/ middle range objectives/ long range goals	general objectives/ particular objectives	interests/ goals/ objectives		interests/ aims/objectives (operations)

TABLE 1 (Continued)

Dimension	Morgenthau[g]	Organski[h]	Van Dyke[i]	Wilkinson[j]	Wolfers[k]
Rank, Status, Involvement	systemwide imperialism/regional/local	dominant nation/great powers/middle powers/small powers/dependencies	maximization of power/indifference to power	first/second/third parties	
Policy Toward Change	status quo/imperialism	"satisfied" (status quo)/"dissatisfied" (change)	satiated/unsatiated states/status quo/revisionist	objectives of political order/policies of political power	status quo/revisionist; national self-extension/national self-preservation/national self-abnegation
Cold War Orientation			aligned/neutral/neutralized/neutralist		U.S.-Soviet Bloc: allies, neutrals, neutralists
Economic Capability		rich/poor	"haves"/"have nots"		
Activity-Passivity		warrior diplomacy/shopkeeper diplomacy	intervention	policies of extension/policies of defense and counterattack	

TABLE 1 (Continued)

Dimension	Morgenthau[g]	Organski[h]	Van Dyke[i]	Wilkinson[j]	Wolfers[k]
Affect			power/welfare	mediator/independent/neutral/isolate/provocateur	amity/enmity;active cooepration/inward-oriented cooperation/minimal amity/competition/minimal enmity/diplomatic enmity
Normative-Motivational	realist/	national goals/humanitarian goals	realism (national self-interest)/utopianism (national idealism)		"possession goal"; "milieu goals"; realist/idealist
Form/Substance	prestige	actual goals/stated goals	pride	real policies/policies of image or prestige	
Hierarchy of Goal		competitive/absolute goals; long range/immediate goals/general/specific goals	vital interests	reactive/militant; goals (strategic objectives)/tactical objectives/"general line of policy"	"hopes"/"goals or vital interests" revolutionary or ideological (universal) goals/tradictional goals; direct goals/indirect goals

a. Coplin (1971)
b. Holsti (1967)
c. Kulski (1968)
d. Lerche and Said (1963)
e. London (1968, 1965)
f. Modelski (1962)

g. Morgenthau (1967)
h. Organski (1968)
i. Van Dyke (1966)
j. Wilkinson (1969)
k. Wolfers (1962)

framework which tells us where and at what to look in order to gather data. In effect, an ad hoc typology seeks to handle the problem of getting "the raw data classified in some reasonable preliminary way, so that it can be communicated, cross-tabulated, and thought about" (Lazarsfeld and Barton, 1955: 24).

Although both definitional and ad hoc typologies are formulated on the basis of the investigator's a priori assumptions about the distinguishing features of international behavior, only ad hoc typologies are constructed by procedures which are explicitly operational, so that the classes they distinguish have readily identifiable empirical referents defined in terms of observables. Further, the two kinds of typologies differ in their purposes. Definitional typologies are devised for the sole purpose of conceptualization, so that communication and speculative explanation may commence; ad hoc typologies, on the other hand, are devised primarily for the purpose of providing categories with which observed behavior can be classified, so that the frequency of occurrences of each specific type of behavior can be calculated.

Since the categories in ad hoc typologies must be operational, they are created to generate quantitative data regarding the number of instances of specified classes of external behavior that occur under specified conditions. Systematic classification with such schemes does not constitute a theory of foreign policy, but logically, ad hoc typologies "stand between theory and the test of theory" (Winch, 1947: 68) because they serve as the mechanism by which data may be acquired, quantified, ordered, and made ready for theorizing. Once the data have been systematically sorted into mutually exclusive classes, it is then possible to devise theoretical explanations of the variations in the categories. But first, ad hoc typologies must be constructed to organize the complex data of external behavior in a meaningful and comparative way.

To date there have been few attempts to construct ad hoc typologies for the systematic collection of data by replicable procedures. And until recently, constructed typologies capable of generating data relevant to the study of foreign policy output were nonexistent. However, the advent of the behavioral movement in political science stimulated efforts to develop categorization schemes for the systematic collection of data, and some of these strivings ultimately bore fruit in producing perceptual (Holsti et al., 1968), transactional (Deutsch et al., 1957), and attribute (Rummel, 1963) data related to the behavior of nations. More recently, a number of taxonomic frameworks have been devised for the collection of data explicitly applicable to the study of foreign policy output behavior (Young and Martin, 1968).[3] These generally fall under the rubric of "events" data. Exemplary of this effort are the ad hoc schemes of McClelland (1967), Leng and Singer (1970), Hermann (1972), Puchala (1969b), and Azar (1970).

The development of such schemes has made the quantitative analysis of foreign policy feasible. Table 2 (pp. 24-25) is an example of one such scheme.

(C) Empirical typologies. Empirical typologies depart from the world of assumed differences and variability between kinds of foreign postures for a world in which the delineation of types is tested for the degree to which the distinctions in national outputs manifest empirical variations. In other words, the postulated a priori categories of international conduct formed by the impressions of the individual are replaced by a taxonomy of foreign policy that is empirically demonstrated to exist (McKinney, 1966: 16, 49-52).[4] As Krieger (1944: 280-288) put it, the types identified by empirical typologies

> differ from all other so-called types in that the cohesiveness of their elements has been proved through the use of . . . data rather than simply supposed through a variety of assumptions.

And Kretschmer (1925: 18-19), who developed an empirical typology of body types, has elaborated that what makes empirical typologies distinctive is that

> The types . . . are not "ideal types" which have emerged, consciously created in accordance with any given guiding principle or collection of pre-existing values. They are, on the contrary, obtained from empirical sources . . . [so that the] description of types . . . refers to . . . characteristics which . . . can be empirically demonstrated.

Logically, empirical typologies are of necessity built from the categories and data collected through ad hoc typologies. That is, ad hoc classificatory schemes provide the basis for empirical schemes because to build an empirically grounded typology one must utilize the categories of ad hoc typologies (Kretschmer, 1925; Krieger, 1944: 273; Winch, 1947: 69-71; Selvin and Hagstrom, 1963: 408-410). Recognizing the nexus between the two, methodologists have by convention come to refer to the process of producing an empirical typology by demonstrating the basis of the ad hoc one through cross-classification of variables as "substruction" (Barton, 1955: 50). Alternately, because the empirical typology is grounded on the observations of the ad hoc scheme, it is sometimes referred to as consisting of "extracted types" (McKinney, 1966) or the "reconceptualization" or "respecification of a concept" (Goode and Hatt, 1958: 48-49). An empirical typology thus seeks to determine if the classes of ad hoc schemes do indeed constitute unitary patterns. Rummel (1970: 1) has described this task of empirical typology construction thusly:

> The problem . . . is that the rationale underlying the categorization [of ad hoc schemes] is often not explicit. It is not clear whether our types really divide different kinds of variance. If we are to deal in types, a clear and empirical basis for the distinctions must be made, such as the variance within each of our groups being less than the variance between our groups.

Therefore the objective of empirical classification is to revise our ad hoc categorizations so as to discover "universal categories" or "natural classes." Winch (1947: 71) has summarized the role of empirical typologies in this process by noting that they can

> (a) correct errors in heuristic [ad hoc] types; (b) reveal types where none has been posited or suspected; and (c) provide a basis for "integrating" various disciplines (by "integration" is meant an empirical demonstration of association between data of various levels of conceptualization plus a "meaningful" interpretation of this relation).

Wood (1969: 238) similarly suggests that empirical typologies, by combining the diverse characteristics inherent in ad hoc categorizations into more homogeneous classes, perform the following useful functions:

> they (1) facilitate serendipitous discovery; (2) provide factual bases for theory construction; (3) suggest explanations for modal types; and (4) can furnish specific evidence for the relative contributions of competing theories.

Hence the rationale for empirical typology construction is rather axiomatic. It is only through scientific research procedures that we are able to discover the "natural structure of social reality." The characteristics of and requirements for such scientific typologies may be briefly summarized. A nonexhaustive and somewhat overlapping list of some of the salient attributes of natural typologies, listed in no particular order or importance, might include that:

(1) Evidence for the empirical existence of the typology must be provided. The properties of the taxonomy are determined not by arbitrary judgment, but by the empirical relations between observables.

(2) Furthermore, the typology must ultimately specify explicitly which dimensions of the phenomena it purports to break down

into components. The dimensions or set of features employed as the basis of classification must be identified. Should a multi-dimensional classificatory scheme be constructed, the categories should delimit the varieties of each dimension and not mix these different aspects across dimensions (Lazarsfeld and Barton, 1955: 86).

(3) Third, the typology should be both exhaustive and mutually exclusive in the delineation of its distinguishing elements along the dimension specified.

(4) Scientific typologies can only approximate the above requirement because although we can logically expect categories to be mutually exclusive we know that empirically there will tend to be considerable overlap in similarity between classes. An empirical typology nevertheless seeks to establish statistical evidence for the independence of categories by showing that every category clusters elements which are highly related (intercorrelated) and that each is maximally independent of the other categories. This is done precisely by the calculation for coefficients of resemblance of elements in each class; substantial independence is approached when the between-class variance is maximized and the within-class variance is minimized. We therefore are able to generate an estimate of the extent to which the classes delineated really "go together" beyond chance.

(5) This requirement suggests another attribute of scientific typologies: a good empirical taxonomy is capable of ordering (ordinally or preferably intervally) or scaling the classes according to the degree to which they reflect the dimension specified (Rudner, 1966: 35-40). Precision is gained because the typology not only identifies types of the phenomena investigated, but also orders the types isolated along a dimensional continuum; the typology is thus able to measure gradations of the attribute and thereby contribute to quantitative measurement.

(6) In addition, it is generally agreed that a scientific typology should be as parsimonious as possible. The smaller the number of categories, the more "powerful" or descriptive each becomes because the types are capable of subsuming under one homogeneous class many variables or aspects of the phenomenon. The rule of parsimony thus suggests that an empirical taxonomy should consist of the minimally sufficient set of types capable of accounting for as much of the general variability as possible. The most efficient way of looking at the subject is the best. "If we are careful (and lucky)," we can discover a structure of international behavior "between the chaotic and procrustean extremes (between a situation in which overdifferentiation makes comparison impossible, and one in which inappropriate parsimony stretches or chops reality)" (Brody, 1972: 48-49).

(7) Moreover, a scientifically generated typology should be verified. This means that ideally the validity and reliability of the categories should be tested to ensure that the variables which make them up are in fact connected with each other as hypothesized and are not some artifact of the investigator's head or his statistical techniques. Evidence must be presented to show that the categories hypothesized to comprise the typology really exist.

(8) Finally, an empirical typology should be capable of demonstrating its utility. Since the rationale for constructing a taxonomic structure must be in the last analysis its employment in future scientific research for the generation of theory and knowledge about the phenomenon it conceptualizes, it is apparent that the utility of the structure is contingent upon its ability to aid in the formulation of theories. While a typology is not itself a theory it aids in the development of positive theory. The typology divides the variance into theoretically meaningful classes and thereby renders the phenomena ready for comparative research. If the structure has been devised properly (that is, if it meets the above requirements), then we would expect it to serve as a tool for the discovery and refinement of hypotheses, and to enter into many theoretical formulations (Stinchcombe, 1968: 45). How well a typology organizes knowledge depends, therefore, on how well it leads to predictions and scientific explanations (Foa, 1958: 230-234). No matter how empirically persuasive or aesthetically appealing a typology may be, ultimately we must judge it on the basis of the contribution it makes to the advancement of reliable knowledge. Our final requirement for a typology, therefore, is that it satisfy the pragmatic test: it must work.

An empirical typology of the external behavior of nations would provide an instrument with which cross-national variations in foreign policy outputs could be systematically measured and compared. The prospects for the development of empirical theory about the causes and consequences of the behavior of nations would be enhanced if future researchers had in their possession a confirmed typology of the universal categories of external action, for it has been repeatedly demonstrated (McKinney, 1966) that the natural classes of empirical typologies are the most theoretically relevant and the most potent in producing explanatory generalizations. That is to say, empirical classifications sort out phenomena in the most parsimoniously generalizable manner possible so that the types delineated are likely to be related to a large number of causal variables. The categories may be expected to be associated with many presumed determinants of state behavior and to consequently enter into a large number of general theoretical statements about foreign policy behavior.

We cannot account for state behavior until we are able to describe it (Leng and Singer, 1970: 1), and satisfactory and reliable description depends, in turn, on a prior acquaintance with the way empirical reality is ordered. A typology of external performance which satisfies the requirements we have specified is capable of accurately demonstrating for us how this empirical world of international conduct is structured. It would thus facilitate systematic foreign policy theory development by empirically identifying the most meaningful set of dimensions with which external behavior can be described, and by providing a set of categories for the classification of policy outputs according to national actors' observed behavior.

TECHNIQUES OF EMPIRICAL TYPOLOGY CONSTRUCTION: THE GUTTMAN CIRCUMPLEX

As we have noted, the problem of discovering empirically verifiable concepts for categorizing external conduct remains essentially unsolved. Part of the difficulty of generating an empirically derived typology capable of measuring foreign policy outputs stems from the lack of any self-evident and compelling methodological procedures for taxonomic construction. Techniques for typology formation have not been devised which are readily agreed on by methodologists, so that a variety of taxonomic practices exist in performing the classificatory task (Sokal and Sneath, 1963: 1-36). As Lazarsfeld and Barton (1951: 82) have noted:

> It can properly be argued that one cannot lay down a set of handy instructions for the categorization of social phenomena; such instructions would be nothing less than a general program for the development of social theory. One cannot write a handbook on how to form fruitful concepts in the same way that one writes handbooks on how to sample or how to construct questionnaires.

Although no explicit universal procedural rules exist for developing meaningful empirical behavioral typologies, scientific methodology does recognize certain essential ground rules for the discovery and formation of types. Most basic to scientific method is that the process of discovering types entail, at a minimum, the application of statistical techniques to estimate how well the types are substantiated. As Lazarsfeld (1962: 470) has put it, "One cannot say two sentences about classificatory procedures in the social sciences without introducing probability notions."

With characteristic lucidity Cattell (1950: 9-10) has described the utility of statistical treatment in typology formation thusly:

The problem of deciding on types is that of detecting the *patterns of concurrent trait endowments which are most frequent.* One cannot make types by fiat; one has to discover them by statistical examination of the population or by the good memory that is a temporary substitute for statistics. . . . Statistical analysis is a device to bring out relationships and patterns which unaided observation and memory could not provide. It does for the mind, struggling in an unfocused chaos of facts, what the microscope does for the unaided eye.

By convention in typological research, the most useful and widely employed statistic for reducing an ad hoc category system to an empirical one has been the simple correlation coefficient. That is, to group the overlapping classes of ad hoc categories into an empirical typology, one capable of discriminating differences in the empirical meaning of the terms, it is necessary to cross-classify or subsume these diverse terms under generic concepts in such a way as to discern which terms are most similar to each other and which are not. The assumption of many methodologists is that for this goal the pattern of intercorrelations of each class with all other classes may be the most important source of information (LaForge and Suczek, 1957: 460). To formulate classificatory concepts, experience suggests, we may ask "whether the patterns of covariation we observe may tell us something about the defining nature of a concept" (Lazarsfeld and Henry, 1968: 3). Basically, the procedure rests on the assumption that:

To the extent that a given class of behavior, x, covaries with another class of behavior, y, the two classes of behavior share common elements. . . . The basic operation employed in the estimation of such behavioral covariation is the well-known coefficient of correlation. Thus, if instances of two classes of behavior are observed to covary . . . the two classes of behavior are assumed to be equivalent and may therefore be "collapsed" into a single class [Carson, 1969: 95].

Beyond this general recommendation for the use of correlational analysis for typology construction, however, no consensus seems to have emerged as to which of the many competing mathematical models (Sokal and Sneath, 1963) are most appropriate for empirical typology formation.

Given the lack of any clear-cut and compelling methodological solution to the problem of devising a meaningful empirical taxonomy of foreign policy behavior, it seems prudent to investigate how other, more advanced analogous behavioral disciplines have sought to resolve their typological measurement problems. That is, the statistical techniques for concept formation employed by developed cognate fields of inquiry may be used for the heuristic purpose of suggesting possible statistical models available for the construction of a typology of the forms of state behavior. Since we possess no multivariate typological procedures uniquely suited to the analysis of external performance data, and since the prospects for the creation of such innovative techniques are not at the moment auspicious, the most advisable course would seem to be to extrapolate existing and proven methods of typology formation presently utilized in related disciplines and apply them to the field of foreign policy (Brody, 1972: 55-56).

The field of interpersonal relations is one such discipline which has given extensive attention to the problem of typology construction, and their experience suggests that a compelling model may exist. The methodological techniques employed for the purpose of discovering the typological structure of interpersonal behavior stem primarily from the work of Guttman (1954: 258-348) and his pioneering radex theory, although numerous modifications and adaptions of this statistical model for the analysis of the interrelationships of a set of concepts have been made. Guttman recognized, along with most methodologists (Winch, 1947: 68-75; Rummel, 1967: 450), that the task of typology construction or concept formation was a job for factor analysis because that technique is capable of reducing a large number of variables to the minimum number of clusters (types) necessary to account for the principal relationships existing among those variables. In this way distinct types are found which group together beyond mere chance. But Guttman also felt that a good typology should do more than merely identify the principal components by which phenomena can be differentiated; he believed that if a systematic set of relationships among the concepts delineated could be demonstrated, the scientific utility of the classificatory scheme would be enhanced. For this improvement he felt it necessary to develop "radex theory," which he termed "a new approach to factor analysis."

A radex, according to Guttman, refers to a general order pattern for the intercorrelations among a set of variables; the word was "designed to indicate a 'radial expansion of complexity' " (Guttman, 1954: 260). It consists of two components, the simplex—which is not relevant to typological construction—and the circumplex model—which is. Basically, a circumplex is designed to order data arrayed in a matrix of intercorrelated variables, that is, sets of product-moment correlation coefficients, in a peculiar way. As Guttman (1954: 325) described it,

> Is it possible to have an ordering without a head and foot to it? Yes, quite simply by having it circular. Then the order has neither

beginning nor end. All variables have an equal rank, but still there is a law of neighboring that holds. A system of variables which has a circular law of order is a circumplex.

Since the purpose of an empirical typology is to discover concepts which cluster variables on the basis of the extent to which they share attributes (as measured by their covariation), it is apparent why the circumplex model is suited to this function. Guttman (1954: 347-348) is explicit in his espousal of the circumplex for this purpose:

> the circumplex seems to be the first example of structures for factor analysis with a law of order which makes the role of principal components unmistakably important.

Because the circumplex defines concepts by virtue of the fact that it is "based on the principles of contiguity and of combinability-separability of discernible elementary components" (Guttman, 1954: 340), it thus is invaluable in typology construction; by uncovering the basic empirical concepts by which a behavioral phenomena may be distinguished, and ordering those concepts in a meaningful way so that their interrelationships may be revealed, the circumplex model may be said to accomplish in an objective fashion the typological task.

Since Guttman formulated his typological model, it has been applied to a wide range of behavioral domains (Carson, 1969; Kegley, 1971; Leary, 1957). The repeated successes of these endeavors in identifying the fundamental dimensions and types of various levels of social behavior suggests that it would be worthwhile to ascertain if the circumplex is capable of discovering an order to the domain of foreign policy behavior as well. A respected international relations theorist, Richard Brody (1972: 54-57), has recommended that the application of the circumplex model to interstate action data might prove fruitful. Hence we will attempt to employ Guttman's model to foreign policy data[6] in order to see if a circumplicial typological ordering of that behavior can be found.

DATA SOURCE

Quantified data about the behavior nations direct to each other are not abundant. One of the most ambitious and comprehensive data sets dealing with this activity is the World Event/Interaction Survey (WEIS), which was collected under the direction of Charles A. McClelland at the University of Southern California. It is this systematically collected body of evidence about internation interactions which we will employ for our typological task.

Although the WEIS data has a number of defects (McClelland, 1968b; Kegley, 1972a), most of which center on problems of validity, nevertheless the source may be considered a reasonable albeit imperfect data base for estimating what international interactions are occurring; in effect, it samples the international behavior that is being undertaken throughout the entire international system. Given the fact that we can never know everything that is occurring, it is pointless to try and observe all international events, so "students of international relations have little alternative but to use the materials at hand with an awareness of their defects" (McClelland, 1968a: 164).

Two other considerations motivate selection of this data set. The first is that properly treated the WEIS collection provides us with an explicit conceptual definition of what we mean by foreign policy output behavior. There are no agreed-upon defining attributes of foreign policy phenomena, so that what activities may properly be regarded as falling under the rubric of "state behavior" vary widely among observers and are thus a frequent source of conceptual contention. The competing conceptions of foreign policy are so varied that one scholar has disparingly noted that "no agreement exists on the meaning of foreign policy" (Hermann, 1972: 22). The WEIS system is attractive because it employs an explicit conceptual definition of foreign policy behavior (McClelland, 1968a; 1969; 1970; McClelland and Hoggard, 1969; Kegley, 1971: 114-143).

Secondly, the WEIS data is attractive because the WEIS interaction categories provide us with an ad hoc typology of foreign policy activity, which segregates the kinds of foreign policy acts (transitive verbs) states may initiate into a set of 63 mutually exclusive and exhaustive categories. This classification system consists, on the basis of intuition, experience, and theory (McClelland, 1970: 29-38; 1968a: 166-169), of the type of actions that may be posited as constituting the major types of behavior by which the activities of national governments abroad may be differentiated and distinguished. Each of the 63 action categories is assumed to be qualitatively different from the others. The WEIS system thus is a suggestive checklist of generic terms, conforming to the language employed by the *New York Times* (McClelland, 1968a: 168), which can be used to classify the almost infinite list of behavioral adjectives that exist for describing foreign conduct. As McClelland and Ancoli (1970: 5) comment:

> The WEIS system permits us to categorize every recorded international act in one of 63 possible classes. This says, in effect, that there are 63 different ways a government can act toward another government. Various combined groupings of the 63 types are used;

TABLE 2
The World Event/Interaction Survey Category System

1. YIELD

011 Surrender, yield to order, submit to order, submit to arrest, etc.

012 Yield position; retreat; evacuate

013 Admit wrongdoing; retract statement

2. COMMENT

021 Explicit decline to comment

022 Comment on situation—pessimistic

023 Comment on situation—neutral

024 Comment on situation—optimistic

025 Explain policy or future position

3. CONSULT

031 Meet with; at neutral site; or send note; stay in same place

032 Visit; go to; leave country

033 Receive visit; host

4. APPROVE

041 Praise, hail, applaud, condolences, ceremonial greetings, thanks

042 Endorse others' policy or position, give verbal support

5. PROMISE

051 Promise own policy support

052 Promise material support

053 Promise other future support action

054 Assure; reassure

6. GRANT

061 Express regret; apologize

062 Give state invitation

063 Grant asylum

064 Grant privilege, diplomatic recognition; de facto relations, etc.

065 Suspend negative sanctions; truce

066 Release and/or return persons or property

7. REWARD

071 Extend economic aid (gift and/or loan)

072 Extend military assistance; joint military exercises

073 Give other assistance

8. AGREE

081 Make substantive agreement

082 Agree to future action or procedure; agree to meet, to negotiate, accept state invitation

9. REQUEST

091 Ask for information

092 Ask for policy assistance; seek

093 Ask for material assistance

094 Request action; call for; ask for asylum

095 Entreat; plead for; appeal to; help

10. PROPOSE

101 Offer proposal

102 Urge or suggest action or policy

11. REJECT

111 Turn down proposal; reject protest demand, threat, etc.

112 Refuse; oppose; refuse to allow; exclude

12. ACCUSE

121 Charge; criticize; blame; disapprove

122 Denounce; denigrate; abuse; condemn

13. PROTEST

131 Make complaint (not formal)

132 Make formal complaint or protest

14. DENY

141 Deny an accusation

142 Deny an attributed policy, action, role, or position

15. DEMAND

150 Issue order or command, insist; demand compliance, etc.

16. WARN

160 Give warning

17. THREATEN

171 Threat without specific negative sanctions

172 Threat with specific nonmilitary negative sanctions

TABLE 2 (Continued)

17. *THREATEN (continued)*	20. *EXPEL*
173 Threat with force specified	201 Order personnel out of country; deport
174 Ultimatum; threat with negative sanctions and time limit specified	202 Expel organization or group
18. *DEMONSTRATE*	21. *SEIZE*
181 Nonmilitary demonstration; walk out on; boycott	211 Seize position or possessions
182 Armed force mobilization, exercise, and/or display	212 Detain or arrest person(s)
	22. *FORCE*
	221 Noninjury destructive act, bomb with no one hurt
19. *REDUCE RELATIONSHIP (as Neg. Sanction)*	222 Nonmilitary injury-destruction
191 Cancel or postpone planned event	223 Military engagement
192 Reduce routine international activity; recall officials, etc.	
193 Reduce or suspend aid or assistance	
194 Halt negotiations	
195 Break diplomatic relations	

the most common of these is a category system consisting of 22 basic types of acts.

Hence, the WEIS coding scheme consists of an ad hoc set of types or cue words for identifying and coding the kinds of behavior that states may take. The advantage of this ad hoc category system is that it provides us with a basis from which an empirical typology may be substructed. The 22 major categories, and the 63 subcategories that are grouped under these headings, are listed in Table 2.

At the risk of being redundant, we should recall that an ad hoc scheme such as WEIS is merely a suggestive way of classifying the types of external conduct; it has been postulated on a priori grounds as a mutually exclusive and exhaustive way of differentiating the variety of forms international behavior may take. Whether this is actually a safe assumption cannot be known without confirmation through construction of an empirical typology, for, as McClelland and Hoggard (1969: 713) warn, "The categories have been regarded initially as separate variables whose independence from one another has been assumed until analysis of the data indicate otherwise." But, for expediency, we will assume that the WEIS categories provide a useful way of classifying and operationalizing foreign policy acts, so that we will build an empirically grounded typology by utilizing the ad hoc nominal categories of the WEIS scheme. This is an appropriate procedure if it is recalled that all empirical typologies must be built from ad hoc ones like the WEIS system (Wood, 1969: 237).

DIMENSIONS OF THE STUDY AND VARIABLE TREATMENT

TEMPORAL BOUNDARIES

The time period with which we will be working consists of the 44 months from January 1966, through August 1969, which covers the temporal segment of the WEIS data which was available at the commencement of this project. By aggregating all the events recorded in this period so as to treat the data as occurring in one temporal span, we are conducting a syncratic, time-point study of foreign policy. Although the decision to regard this era as a single time period is admittedly arbitrary, analysis is contingent upon some periodization and it may be submitted that a 44-month block is a sufficient but not overlengthy one in which to observe and collect information about international behavior. Other typological studies (Salmore and Munton, 1973; Young, 1970) have employed similar and identical time frames, which enhances the prospects for comparison and replication of results. Assuming that this block of time is representative of other epochs in international history, aggregation and static treatment appears warranted for a study which seeks to describe and measure patterns of foreign policy behavior rather than model the dynamics of internation interaction or the sequences of external stimuli that presumably produce external conduct.

It is axiomatic that if the results of the study are to be generalizable to both past and future, then the behavior observed in our selected time frame must not be of a unique or idiosyncratic sort. The time frame must not be an anomalous one. Unfortunately, sufficient longitudinal data do not presently exist to ascertain the extent to which the pattern of interstate behavior associated with different international systems varies over time (Kegley, 1972a). Consequently, the effort to select a time period that is as typical or normal as possible, so that the resultant empirical typology of foreign policy is not bound by time for its validity, is a rather subjective exercise.

Nevertheless, face support for the typicality of our 44-month period may be found in the observation that no abnormal international situations occurred in this time span, such as a major war, which might contaminate the data that were not at least partially controlled for by the WEIS coding procedures (McClelland and Hoggard, 1969: 713). For instance, the coding rules prevented events associated with Vietnam and the June 1967 war in the Middle East from dominating the data collection and thereby biasing the kind of external conduct reported.

Moreover, preliminary analysis of the data for this period reveals that the monthly volume of foreign policy activity recorded in the collection is highly stable (Kegley, 1971: 185-195; Hill, 1971). Calculation of the central tendencies of the monthly frequency distributions shows a mean frequency of 521.9 acts per month (median = 515; mode = 525); and, measuring dispersion, we find that the standard deviation of the monthly distributions is 122.6. These figures suggest that the flow of foreign policy events in the time period selected for study does not fluctuate widely. If we accept McClelland's (1969; 1972) contention that changes in the behavioral characteristics of the international system may be ascertained by fluctuations in the amount of international activity pursued by states, so that marked variations in the quantity of recorded events may be interpreted as indicative of an interstate system that is undergoing transformation, then it follows that the absence of extreme fluctuation suggests that the international system as delimited by our time period is a relatively stable and homogeneous one. This finding further suggests that the behavior we are sampling from the WEIS collection in this period is from a fairly regular international system, one that is representative of normal external conduct rather than peculiar foreign activity emanating from a few unique historical international crises. Thus on inspection it appears that time based errors have been minimized, that our data are not unique to this time period, and that our findings will not be specific to this particular span of history. Additional evidence has elsewhere been accumulated (Kegley, 1972a) which demonstrates that the structure of international behavior is relatively invariant over time, and that it is possible to construct empirical typologies whose classificatory structures are reliable (reproducible) in diverse temporal spans. This should enhance our confidence in the feasibility of empirically deriving temporally reliable general typologies of foreign policy behavior.

NATIONAL ACTOR POPULATION FOR THE STUDY

A second dimension of the study concerns the actors to be included in the analysis. According to our conceptual definition of foreign policy output, we conceive of a particular country's foreign policy not as a summary of the aggregate types of behavior it initiated to all other actors in the international system (monads), but rather in a dyadic fashion as a description of the actions a nation directs to specific national targets. By conceptualizing the lines of a dyadic relationship (what country A does to country B: $A \rightarrow B$) as the basic unit of analysis, it is axiomatic that we must select for study directed dyads for which there is a sufficient amount of data (interactions) to permit meaningful statistical analysis. Examination of these and other data (Kegley, 1972b) on interactions between pairs of states informs us that a relatively few number of dyads account for a large proportion of the total international activity. This means, empirically, that most states are very selective in their attention to other states, concentrating their behavior on a relatively small number of targets. (The evidence for these conclusions is summarized in Appendix A.)

The consequence of this distribution of interaction activity between states is that if we hope to build a typology of foreign policy behavior, we must sample so as to include in our study only those dyads with a meaningful volume of interaction between partners. Somewhat arbitrarily (Kegley, 1971: 213-220), we define a meaningful dyadic foreign policy relationship as one in which a national actor is observed to interact at least five times in our sample period with another national actor. This sampling decision rule produced a sample population of 91 states, which formed a total of 452 meaningful directed dyads (5 acts) and possessed in the aggregate 11,007 acts which is 81 percent of all *interstate* acts in the data set. Since these 452 directed dyads account for such a large proportion of the interstate activity, we assume that we have identified the core of the international system and that retention of these 452 dyads for study is warranted. The 452 will thus constitute our sample. (This sample population of 452 dyads is listed in Appendix B.)

BEHAVIORAL VARIABLES IN THE STUDY

Perusal of the distributions of the 22 major categories of international activity in the WEIS system indicates that there is much variation in the frequency with which these various ad hoc types of action are undertaken in the international system. Figure 1 illustrates this variation across behavioral types.

Because the data as organized by the 22 provisional WEIS categories are found to cluster in a few predominant classes, a reformulation of the 63 WEIS categories is called for (Kegley, 1971: 195-203; Salmore and Munton, 1973; McGowan, 1972). What criteria should be employed to formulate a new set of categories for foreign behavior from the original 63? At a minimum, we will seek to retain the arrangement of the 63 action types in the 22 categories wherever possible, because for theoretical and intuitive reasons they cluster together. There is some empirical evidence (McClelland and Hoggard, 1969; Salmore and Salmore, 1970; Young, 1970) that they form a composite, a functional unity, in sharing common characteristics. Secondly, we will maintain the ordering of the types along the posited conflict-cooperation continuum, so that categories will be

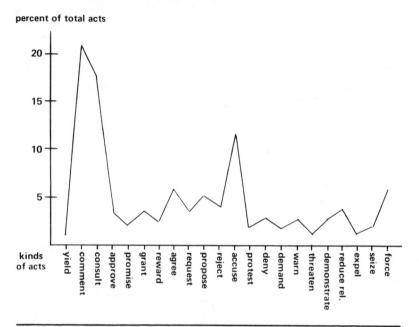

Percentage Distribution, By 22 Basic Types,
of the Total WEIS Data

Figure 1: VARIATION ACROSS BEHAVIORAL TYPES

combined or collapsed only with adjacent associated categories (that is, following Barton's [1955: 40-45] recommendation categories will be combined which are proximate in the degree to which they resemble each other along the hypothesized dimensional attribute). Theoretically, this should ensure that the combined types constitute as homogeneous a class as possible. Our third rule for devising a revised category system will require, so as to eliminate categories with too few cases, that each type contain no less than 1.7 percent of the total cases. This is an admittedly arbitrary, but necessary, minimal requirement which will ensure that a sufficient number of cases will exist in each category to make it meaningful (in the sense that each type will possess empirical referents). It should be noted that in this process no WEIS categories have been deleted from the set; all have either remained independent or been combined with other contiguous categories to form a new type. And finally, we will as a fourth rule disaggregate any "combevent" type (combination of event types) into the maximum number of available WEIS subtypes which we can without violating our previous requirement that the resultant types comprise an adequate proportion of the total number of cases (1.7%). This decision is motivated by the assumption that the present combevent categories possessing a disproportionate percentage of cases are not sufficiently homogeneous to remain discrete classes, and that they can, therefore, be safely subdivided into a number of distinct meaningful categories.

Examining the data for the 63 types of foreign behavior, and following the above rules, therefore produces a revised category system consisting of 24 classes. This set is listed in Table 3, and is accompanied by the frequency and percentage for each type of act. The relative proportion of acts accruing to each of the categories may now be summarized, for comparative purposes, in Figure 2. As can be readily observed, this revised set of categories for international action produces a much more uniform distribution across the categories than did the 22 WEIS combevent categories. (The distributional characteristics of these 24 foreign policy output variables are summarized in Appendix C.) The frequency of the 24 types now ranges from 400 to 2639 (400 instances of yield behavior to 2639 instances of comment action). The mean frequency has been reduced from 1043.9 to 956.9, and, more significantly, the dispersion as measured by the standard deviation is now only 607.7 (versus 1227.4 previously). Thus, by rearranging and combining the 63 WEIS categories into a new typology, we eliminate nonsignificant types and arrive at a statistically meaningful way of categorizing foreign policy output without violating the actual patterns in the data. The categories remain ordered along a hypothetical conflict-cooperation continuum, and although there are now 15 categories of a more or less cooperative type vis-à-vis 9 categories of a conflictual nature, the proportion of conflictual acts remains approximately the same (29% conflictual versus 32% previously). Thus this revised category scheme of the types of acts nations initiate does not appear to have significantly distorted the data, and will therefore be employed throughout the remainder of the study.

THE STRUCTURE OF FOREIGN POLICY OUTPUTS:
AN EMPIRICAL TEST OF THE CIRCUMPLEX MODEL

SEARCHING FOR A CIRCUMPLEX CONFIGURATION:
A FIRST PROBE OF THE DATA

As the previous discussion has suggested, there are two principal methods for testing for the existence of a circumplicial order of concepts.

TABLE 3

Twenty-Four General Categories of Foreign Policy Behavior Derived
from 63 WEIS Types of Action, with Frequencies, for Total WEIS
Collection, January 1966-August 1969

Category	WEIS Derivation[a]	Frequency	%
Yield	011 + 012 + 013 + 021 +022	400	1.74
Comment	023	2639	11.49
Explain	024 + 025	2088	9.09
Meet	031	1140	4.96
Visit	032	1416	6.17
Host	033	1407	6.13
Approve	041 + 042	770	3.35
Promise	051 + 052 + 053 + 054	456	1.99
Grant	061 + 062 + 063 + 064 + 065 + 066	867	3.78
Reward	071 + 072 + 073	677	2.95
Substantive agreement	081	749	3.26
Agree to meet	082	728	3.17
Request	091 + 092 + 093 + 094 + 095	880	3.83
Offer	101	418	1.82
Urge	102	783	3.41
Reject	111 + 112	802	3.40
Charge	121	2277	9.92
Protest	122 + 131 + 132	709	3.09
Deny	141 + 142	464	2.02
Issue warning	150 + 160	677	2.95
Threatening display	171 + 172 + 173 + 174 + 181 + 182	554	2.41
Reduce relation-ship	191 + 192 + 193 + 194 + 195	433	1.89
Expel-seize	201 + 202 + 211 +212	1138	4.96
Force	221 + 222 + 223	1138	4.96

n = 63 classes for foreign action

n = 22965 acts

a. Consult Table 2 for a listing of the code system for the WEIS categories.

Both have been widely employed. The first involves inspection and
arrangement of the intercorrelation matrix for the variables investigated.
Because measures of association or concomitant variation are able to
inform us of the relative contiguity, similarity, and remoteness of a set of
variables, they provide us with a means of determining whether our
conceptually distinct variables are empirically distinct. By enabling us to
ascertain empirically the extent to which variables resemble one another
and may be differentiated, correlational procedures serve as an indis-
pensable aid in typology construction. As Lazarsfeld (1937: 120) has

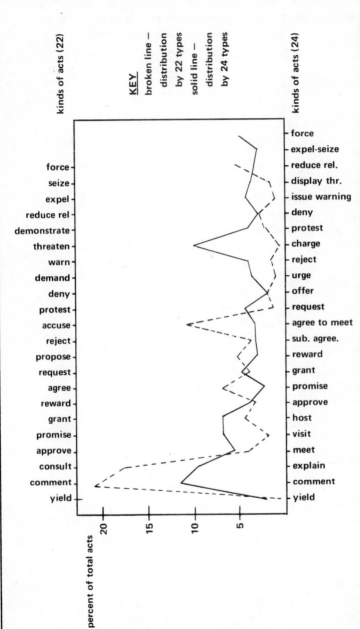

percent of total acts

kinds of acts (22)

KEY
broken line — distribution by 22 types
solid line — distribution by 24 types

kinds of acts (24)

Figure 2: PERCENTAGE DISTRIBUTION, BY REVISED SET OF 24 TYPES OF FOREIGN POLICY ACTIVITY, FOR TOTAL WEIS DATA

noted, a "type" is essentially little more than a plurality or correlated characteristics. Hence, for our purposes the empirical intercorrelation of our output variables is invaluable information, indicating to us the conceptual interrelationship of our variables and allowing us to thereby determine comparatively which variables have the most in common.

To test for the existence of a postulated circular rank order among the variables, Guttman suggested correlating each variable with every other and then rearranging the sequence of the variables to determine if the resultant correlation matrix will fit the typical circumplicial pattern. Guttman (1954: 329) described the distinguishing characteristics of this pattern thusly:

> There will be a tendency for the largest correlations to be next to the main diagonal and in the upper-right and lower-left corners ... but this will only be a tendency and not a strict rule. ... There is an unmistakable trend for the largest correlations, ...to taper off as they depart from the (main) diagonal, and then to increase again at the northeast and southwest corners.

Thus, the matrix of intercorrelations in the perfect circumplex has a characteristic arrangement. Lorr and McNair (1965: 824) have described this array lucidly:

> In a correlation matrix exhibiting a circular order, the highest correlations are next to the principal diagonal which runs from the upper left to the lower right corner. Along any row (or column) the correlations decrease in size as one moves further away from the main diagonal and then increases again ... the correlations of any specified variable with its neighbors decrease monotonically in size and then increase monotonically as a function of their sequential separation. Contiguous variables correlate positively while more distant variables correlate close to zero.

Table 4 illustrates how a hypothetical perfect circumplex would appear.

Hence the hypothesis of a circular rank order may be tested through correlational analysis. When the relative sizes of the statistical coefficients can be ordered into the circumplicial order, then the hypothesis of a circular order is confirmed.

Employing Pearson's r (Guttman, 1954: 260; Kegley, 1971: 254-257)[7] to the 24 foreign policy output variables, in order to determine the degree of covariation between all possible pairs of variables, produced an intercorrelation matrix which is presented in Table 5. Note that the variables were rearranged so as to achieve the best approximate fit to the anticipated circumplex pattern. The result, as is apparent from an

TABLE 4
Intercorrelations for an Equally Spaced, Uniform, Perfect,
Additive Circumplex

Variable	V_1	V_2	V_3	V_4	V_5	V_6
V_1	1.00	.75	.50	.25	.50	.75
V_2	.75	1.00	.75	.50	.25	.50
V_3	.50	.75	1.00	.75	.50	.25
V_4	.25	.50	.75	1.00	.75	.50
V_5	.50	.25	.50	.75	1.00	.75
V_6	.75	.50	.25	.50	.75	1.00
Total	3.75	3.75	3.75	3.75	3.75	3.75

a. Summed correlations are meaningless statistically. They are placed here to indicate the similarities of columns.

examination of the resultant matrix, is pleasantly clear: the relative patterning of the size of the coefficients indicates the presence of a circular rank ordering of the variables. To be sure, our matrix reveals neither a perfect circumplex nor an equally spaced one; there are some conspicuous deviations from the predicted pattern, and the gradient of increase of the coefficients varies considerably for different variables. In some portions of the matrix correlations are obtained which are inconsistent with their position, and in other parts of the sequence deviations from monotonicity occur. But nevertheless, the matrix suggests, unmistakably, the existence of a circumplex pattern. That is, the circumplicial law of order among the variables does seem to hold, in that: (1) the largest correlations tend to cluster along the main diagonal and in the extreme left-hand corner; (2) there is a concomitant tendency for the magnitudes of the coefficients to decrease as we move away from the main diagonal and to increase again as the corner is approached; and (3) the correlations between contiguous variables are for the most part higher than those that obtain between more distant variables. Although some conspicuous deviations and variations from this pattern occur, they are not systematic, and we are thus led to conclude that because our matrix for the most part obeys these rules of order support for the hypothesis of the circumplex structure has been found. As Guttman (1954) pointed out, evidence for a circumplicial configuration may be obtained with rather severe deviations from a perfect additive arrangement.

Our data have afforded us the opportunity to approximate, therefore, what Guttman (1954: 329) has termed a "quasi-circumplex" formation. It deviates from the perfect circumplex, or "circulant" order, in that neither

TABLE 5
Intercorrelation Matrix of 24 Foriegn Policy Output Variables Arranged in Quasi-Circumplex Order[a]

	17	18	20	16	3	2	4	15	14	13	9	19	12	1	11	7	6	8	5	10	24	21	22	23
17—Charge	100																							
18—Protest	75	100																						
20—Issue Warning	74	78	100																					
16—Reject	69	75	76	100																				
3—Explain	48	50	63	69	100																			
2—Comment	51	54	56	65	65	100																		
4—Meet	40	39	50	59	62	77	100																	
15—urge	74	45	58	60	65	65	70	100																
14—Offer	48	51	70	62	65	57	64	77	100															
13—Request	35	36	47	51	59	59	51	75	75	100														
9—Grant	48	44	56	56	55	44	50	44	56	49	100													
19—Deny	48	41	61	53	48	42	49	65	74	61	71	100												
12—Agree to Meet	39	40	39	57	63	70	69	65	39	40	53	54	100											
1—Yield	28	26	32	31	31	46	49	47	39	50	45	50	61	100										
11—Sub. Agree	29	32	36	42	40	63	57	54	36	49	42	28	72	41	100									
7—Approve	20	24	28	34	54	55	48	47	31	49	30	22	62	38	54	100								
6—Host	10	06	11	16	33	31	42	25	07	29	09	01	40	19	43	61	100							
8—Promise	00	09	05	07	24	15	34	20	06	07	09	04	28	45	28	52	36	100						
5—Visit	-02	03	07	06	25	22	41	29	10	10	11	07	38	38	44	57	49	43	100					
10—Reward	-08	-01	00	01	14	12	22	13	03	03	08	02	15	13	21	35	21	49	43	100				
24—Force	37	27	40	23	09	08	07	03	21	20	32	40	37	-15	03	32	20	-07	13	-02	100			
21—Threat. Display	53	26	48	40	33	35	27	32	37	32	34	33	37	25	26	20	03	03	-02	-10	67	100		
22—Reduce Rel.	53	34	11	29	35	38	30	26	19	22	25	15	27	19	18	17	11	04	15	07	34	35	100	
23—Expel-Seize	52	27	55	23	35	50	50	37	31	29	33	30	24	26	34	4	-12	-02	00	-02	32	40	35	100

a. Coefficients have been rounded to two places and multiplied by 100 to remove decimal points.

the correlations between adjacent variables are constant nor are the hierarchical gradients between diagonals parallel to the main diagonal even; but nevertheless the general character of the circumplex pattern is preserved and the arrangement is sufficiently ordered to enable us to submit that the data fit the circumplicial structure of hierarchy among variables. This discovery should thus be considered an encouraging achievement for us, and in no way should be thought of as somehow tarnished because a perfect circumplex was not found. Deviations from the ideal or perfect circumplex, Guttman (1954: 279) advised, should be expected with empirical data. And some solace may be taken in the fact that our circumplicial model of the data compares favorably to other reported circumplex structures, in terms of the extent to which it approximates a perfect circular rank ordering (Guttman, 1954: 330; Lorr and McNair, 1965: 823-830; Schaeffer, 1959: 226-235).

Other than indicating to us the existence of a circumplex order among the variables, the intercorrelation matrix offers in addition some further information about these measures. The coefficients in Table 5 tell us that in general the variables are fairly highly related to each other: 109, or over 40% of the bivariate coefficients, are larger than .50, which indicates rather crudely that most of the variables are strongly associated with many others. On the surface, multicollinearity among variables seems to thus be present, which is suggestive of the possible existence of several highly interdependent—and hence homogeneous—clusters of variables in the data. Because of this empirical covariation or mutual going-togetherness, such clusters if identifiable would go far in enabling us to discern discrete types of variables in a typology.

Furthermore, our intercorrelation matrix reveals that a large proportion (96%) of the pairs of variables are positively associated. Nearly all of them vary in the same direction. This suggests that the variables are related to or are measuring a basic single dimension of foreign policy activity, which presumably is a reflection of the underlying affect continuum on which our variables are hypothetically arrayed. However, the existence of a smaller set of variables which correlates moderately with each other but negatively and very weakly with the other variables instructs us as to the possible presence of a second dimension in the data. But whether several variables are indeed related to such a secondary dimension or concept requires a more thorough probing of the data. We cannot separate clusters clearly or discern their exact boundaries with an instrument as imprecise as our eyeball.

What our quasi-circumplex order informs us of is only the general nature of the circular order of the variables, and not the precise order

(Guttman, 1954: 278-279). What we obtain is merely a rough estimate of the order in which the variables might arrange themselves around the circumference of an imaginary circle if they were to be displayed graphically in that manner (Carson, 1969: 97).[8] But we do not learn from the matrix the exact order; and because the units around the scale are not equidistant we cannot discover the relative degree of separation between the variables, which would have enabled us to infer how similar or different two variables are to each other and with respect to the rest. We only achieve an approximation of this order. Hence there are serious limitations as to what an intercorrelation matrix resembling a quasi-circumplex order can tell us. The quasi-ordered matrix does not lend itself to easy substantive interpretation.

These limitations thus suggest the need for further analysis. Encouraged by the discovery of evidence suggesting the existence of a circular pattern among the variables through inspection of the intercorrelation matrix, we are stimulated to delineate more clearly the characteristics of the circular pattern of the variables. Thus, we follow Guttman's (1954: 279) advice that

> If inspection [of the correlation matrix] reveals a [circumplicial] hierarchy, then the hierarchy exists. Knowing it exists should spur efforts to reveal its nature in more detail, and may perhaps ultimately lead to an exact parametric theory for it.

To further interpret the meaning of the patterns in the correlation matrix requires the use of more sophisticated methods, and for that task we now turn to factor analysis. By extracting from the correlation matrix a number of separate factors or dimensions, factor analysis untangles the pattern of interrelationship among the variables, sorts the variables into distinct (statistically independent) classes, and determines the extent to which each variable is related to these different sources of variation. Hence, because factor analysis is a method which allows us to probe the interrelationships among variables existing in our intercorrelation matrix for the discovery and delineation of distinct patterns of shared variation in the data, it enables us to determine more carefully the extent to which the hypothesis of a circular arrangement of the variables is sustainable. Factor analysis procedures therefore permit us to ascertain whether the original ordering of the variables arrived at through inspection of the intercorrelation matrix alone was warranted, and it enables a more exact specification of the interrelationships of the variables in a circular or other order to be made.

**VERIFYING THE CIRCUMPLEX ARRANGEMENT:
A SECOND PROBE OF THE DATA**

In order to condense our 24 foreign policy output variables into a meaningful number of summary dimensions, the principal components (principal axes) method of factor analysis was applied to the data to discern the underlying patterns of association among the variables (Kegley, 1971: 268-270). Furthermore, an R-technique type of factor analysis was utilized. This type is appropriate when the purpose is to uncover the factors that underlie variables rather than individual cases (dyads). Moreover, it should be noted that squared multiple correlation coefficients were inserted in the principal diagonal of the correlation matrix before extraction (Rummel, 1970: 166; Vincent, 1969: 5-6),[9] and Coomb's criterion (Garson, 1971: 208; Vincent, 1969: 13-14; Rummel, 1970: 349-367)[10] was utilized to determine the number of factors to be extracted. As can be seen from the following factor matrix this rule-of-thumb determined that only two factors were retained, which fits with our intuitive expectations and serves the interests of parsimony, in that we are better off with the smallest number of dimensions which can adequately account for the interrelations among the variables. It seems to be a justifiable criterion, moreover, because an examination of the residuals after extraction of two factors indicated that extraction of a third would have accounted for not even an additional five percent of the total variance; this level of variance is probably below an acceptable limit for descriptive purposes, since it would contain too high a proportion of random error to be meaningful.

It should also be noted that both orthogonally and obliquely rotated factors are presented with the unrotated factor structure that resulted. For this purpose, Kaiser's varimax criterion was applied to create the rotated factors that are orthogonal, whereas an oblique solution was obtained by employing Thurstone's simple structure criteria for rotation to a unique structure. The computational procedures employed utilized the BMD X72 Factor Analysis Program (Dixon, 1968; 1969). The results of the factor analysis are displayed in Table 6.

A number of observations germane to our typological purpose are derivable from this matrix. Prior to interpretation of the nature of the factors we might note characteristics of specific variables as they relate to others by examining the communality (h^2) values for each of the variables in the analysis. Since the communalities indicate to us the proportion of variation of each variable in common with all the others, they may be taken as an indication of the degree to which a variable is related (or unrelated) to the others, that is, how much it is involved in the patterns.

Perusal of the values shows that most of the communalities for the variables are high, suggesting that they hold much in common with the other variables; this implies further that the factors are imparting a good deal of meaning (Rummel, 1963: 11). However, the rather low communalities pertaining to variables 10, 22, and 24 indicate that these may be infused with considerable random error or may contain primarily specific variance. This tells us that they are relatively unique and unrelated to the others. Nevertheless, the general overall strength exhibited by the communalities leads us to condlude that our factors have considerable validity.

Moreover, we might inquire as to the extent to which the total variation in the data is patterned, that is, how much regularity or order there is in the interrelationships among the variables. This was difficult to estimate from inspection of the correlation matrix alone. As can now be clearly seen, the two patterns (factors) we have delineated are alone able to account for over 50% of the total possible variation. This high percentage of variation among all the variables suggests a high degree of uniformity or patterning. Substantively, it tells us that the foreign policy behavior emanating between nations is highly structured behavior, and that the types of acts states initiate across borders demonstrate a high level of resemblance. It indicates that certain combinations of acts tend to co-occur more frequently than certain others. Furthermore, it informs us that there is a great deal of relationship among the variables and that these behavioral patterns can be described with a few basic dimensions. This is, in itself, a nonsurprising but important (Kegley, 1972a: 34-37) finding, lending credence to our intuitive suspicions that external behavior is patterned and can be categorized according to some basic classes of action.

With these points in mind, let us turn to the rotated factor matrix, since, because our aim is to employ factors to formulate classificatory categories, the unrotated matrix is inadequate. The unrotated factors define only the most general components of variance in the data, whereas rotated factors delineate the empirical clusters of relationship among the variables (Rummel, 1967: 471-477). For the purpose of classification, it is the discovery of these distinct clusters of interdependent variables which is germane, for they define generic classificatory concepts under which the variables may be subsumed. Since it is these cluster patterns which we thus seek to find, and not variance, rotation is called for.

To this end, two types of rotation were performed, orthogonal and oblique simple structure. The orthogonal matrix presents us with a dichotomized typology, in that the two factors distinguish two clusters of variables which are completely independent; the correlation between the

TABLE 6
Dimensions of Dyadic Foreign Policy Behavior [a,b]

	Unrotated Factors		Orthogonally Rotated Factors		Obliquely Rotated Factors (Simple Structure)		
	I	II	I	II	I	II	h^2 [c]
20—Issue Warning	78	−39	88	05	90	−12	77
17—Charge	68	−47	82	−06	85	−23	68
16—Reject	79	−27	82	16	84	01	70
18—Protest	69	−42	81	−01	83	−17	65
14—Offer	75	−20	75	20	76	06	61
19—Deny	67	−26	71	10	72	−03	51
9—Grant	69	−16	68	20	69	08	50
15—Urge	82	07	67	47	66	34	67
2—Comment	82	09	66	48	65	36	67
3—Explain	78	05	65	44	65	31	61
23—Expel-Seize	60	−25	65	08	66	−04	33
21—Threat. Display	53	−22	57	07	58	−04	33
13—Request	73	14	56	49	55	38	55
24—Force	27	−42	44	−23	47	−32	25
1—Yield	55	13	41	39	40	32	33
22—Reduce Rel.	39	−08	38	13	38	06	16
7—Approve	62	56	25	80	21	76	70
5—Visit	34	62	−02	70	−06	72	50
6—Host	36	51	06	62	02	62	39
8—Promise	25	52	−04	58	07	59	34
4—Meet	82	31	55	68	53	58	77
11—Sub. Agree	66	34	39	63	37	55	55
12—Agree to Meet	79	25	55	62	52	53	69
10—Reward	17	45	−08	48	−11	50	23
% of Total Variance [d]	40.7		11.8				52.5
% of Common Variance [e]	77.7		22.2		r = .24		99.9
Eigenvalues [f]	9.8		2.8				

a. Loadings have been rounded to two places and multiplied by 100 to remove decimal points.

b. Loadings in bold face to indicate factor on which particular variable loads the highest, variables have been ordered according to the size of their loadings on oblique factors.

c. h^2 = communality of each variable; i.e., sum of squared factor loadings for each variable.

d. Total variance = sum of squares of each factor divided by number of variables.

e. Common variance = sum of squares of each factor divided by sum of column of h^2 values.

f. Eigenvalues = sum of column of squared loadings for each factor.

two factors (defining types) is zero. This means substantively that the variance between the two classes has been maximized, that the classes have been separated conceptually to the greatest extent possible. The similarity between the two factors (classes, types, descriptive categories) has thus in this case been minimized. In the orthogonal case, the factor loadings may be interpreted as they are in the unrotated case (i.e., like r coefficients, so that they may be read to determine the degree of relationship of each variable to the factors identified). The loadings therefore inform us which variables belong or associate most strongly with which factor, allowing us to infer the extent to which each variable is involved in defining the factors. The variables that load highly on a factor form a pattern of interdependent foreign policy acts identified by the factor. They thus tell us about the defining nature of the dimension, what it is describing or classifying.

The effect of rotation to an orthogonal fit is to alter the correlations of the variables with the factors without changing the percentage of variance of each variable being accounted for by both factors. In general, rotation means that (1) the factors no longer necessarily define decreasing amounts of variation in the data, and (2) the factor loadings may be correlated although the factors are not. This latter point is especially important when factor analysis is being employed for typology construction. It means that when orthogonality is obtained the variables may be simultaneously correlated with more than one factor. Thus, while orthogonal rotation achieves the delineation of distinct and independent factors (descriptive classes), it does not ensure that the variables subsumed under each factor are sufficiently interdependent and homogeneous to be regarded as possessing a high degree of similarity on that defining factor. In short, while between-class variance has been maximized in the orthogonal case, there is no guarantee that within-class variance has been concomitantly minimized.

To correct this deficiency, a more precise definition of the variable interrelationships was sought through oblique rotation procedures. What oblique rotation does, in essence, is to rotate the factors individually until each factor is able to delineate as distinct a variable cluster as possible. It seeks the best definition of the uncorrelated and correlated cluster patterns among the variables; "orthogonal rotation defines only uncorrelated patterns [whereas] oblique rotation has greater flexibility in searching out patterns regardless of their correlation" (Rummel, 1967: 467). The factor patterns that are discovered may then be investigated to determine exactly the degree of relationship existing between them (Rummel, 1967: 477). Rummel (1970: 388) has summarized these advantages of oblique vis-à-vis orthogonal rotation for us with characteristic lucidity:

> First, it generates additional information; there is a more precise definition of the boundaries of a cluster, and the central variables in a cluster can be identified by their high loadings. Moreover, information about the correlations constitute substantive knowledge in their own right and enable the researcher to gauge the degree to which his data approximate orthogonal factors. . . . A second ground for justifying oblique rotation is epistemological. It is argued that the world cannot be realistically treated as though basic functional unities represented by the factors are uncorrelated. Phenomena, whether singly or in clusters, are interrelated, and the factors themselves must reflect this reality to be represented by the factor correlations.

Hence, because of its ability to better define clusters of variables and the variables involved in a cluster, oblique rotation appears to be most apt for our taxonomic purposes. It permits us to define distinct types of foreign activity while at the same time maximizing the homogeneity of the variables comprising those types (marking them as collinear as possible).

Calculating the correlation between the two clusters of variables obtained by oblique rotation reveals that we do not gain too much in between-class variance through rotation: the resultant cluster patterns now correlate only slightly (r = .24). This means that the two factor types delineated are nearly orthogonal or conceptually "opposite" after arriving at an oblique fit, which is satisfying; the factor types found continue to differentiate dissimilar dimensions of foreign policy activity. On the other hand, inspection of the factor loadings suggests that oblique rotation has succeeded in augmenting the homogeneity (interdependence) of the variables loading on the separate factors; the within-class variance has been reduced even further and the variables now correlate with but one factor. These observations lead us to conclude, therefore, that our oblique structure provides us with the best or most plausible solution to defining distinct classes of foreign policy behavior. These pleasing properties associated with oblique simple structure rotation[11] thus will make our oblique matrix solution the object of all subsequent interpretation.[12] It forms the basis from which we will derive our empirical typology, since it provides us with the best overall definition of the clusters of our interrelated variables.

The matrix can therefore now be subjected to more substantive interpretation. Inspection of the matrix enables us to attempt to identify and name the two dimensions delineated. This is an admittably judgmental exercise, but one that is not overly arbitrary when a somewhat simple factor structure, such as ours, is emergent.

The most informative clue as to what the factors are describing is the substance of the variables loading highly and nearly zero on each factor (Rummel, 1970: 475-477). Ordering the variables in terms of the size of their loadings on the two factors reveals the following rank (see Table 7).

Some of the variables, however, are rather ambiguous, in that they load rather highly on both classificatory factors. Figure 3 illustrates those variables possessing this characteristic by delineating the variables which load over .30 on both dimensions; variables that unequivocally relate to only one categorical cluster are not shown. Most of these eight variables clearly load most heavily on only one of the factors, and can therefore be placed with ease; only variables 4 (meet) and 12 (agree to meet) loaded rather equally on both factors and were relatively difficult to place. These loadings provide us with additional information about the defining nature of the two factors (classifications), however, enabling us to better interpret their substantive meaning and what they are describing.

From these two above pieces of information we may now venture names for our two factors. Let us submit that Factor I (the most important factor in terms of the variance it accounts for), by the nature of the types of acts loading on it, does seem to be classifying the degree of affect, the level of hostility and friendship, existing in an interactive dyad. It includes virtually all of the conflictual types of acts states may undertake, both military and nonmilitary, and includes as well a portion of less conflictual acts (grant, comment, explain, request, yield). These latter types of acts may generally be characterized as being of a cooperative nature, as defined by the WEIS coding rules. Moreover, we may argue, it makes substantive sense to find these acts clustering together on the same dimension; we would expect a mix of both hostile and friendly acts to be manifested in an active internation dyad. To some extent nations must

TABLE 7
Location of 24 Foreign Policy Output Variables on Two Classificatory Factors

Factor I		Factor II
Issue warning	Comment	Approve
Charge	Explain	Visit
Reject	Expel-seize	Host
Protest	Threatening display	Promise
Offer	Request	Meet
Deny	Force	Substantive agreement
Grant	Yield	Agree to meet
Urge	Reduce relationship	Reward

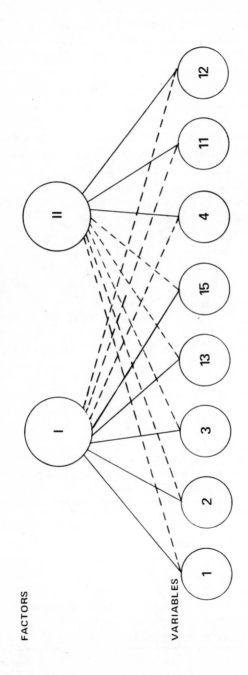

FACTORS

VARIABLES

Solid line indicates factor on which variable loads most heavily and broken line indicates factor with which variable is less strongly involved.

Figure 3: VARIABLES LOADING ON BOTH CLASSES

cooperate in order to conflict, so that it should not be surprising to find both kinds of acts tending to co-occur. Rosenau and Hoggard (1971: 28) have concisely couched this viewpoint when they noted it is

> erroneous to conceive of conflict and cooperation as if they were independent of each other. . . . It is clear that societies which engage in a high (or low) degree of dyadic conflict must also undertake a high (or low) degree of dyadic cooperation in order to sustain their international relationships. Conflict necessitates bargaining and bargaining involves concessions as well as protests, with the result that the more a society is inclined to be conflictful in its dyadic relationships, the more will it also have to be cooperative.

Hence, the first dimension seems to have defined for us in a reasonable way the types of acts we might expect to find evident in a dyadic relationship best described on the conflict-cooperation continuum. The relative higher loadings of the more hostile categories vis-à-vis the cooperative ones fits this interpretation as well, in that the advent of hostile activities between dyad partners may thus be seen as actuating and provoking those more cooperative actions necessary for the maintenance of the relationship. Without a hostile raison d'être the cooperative acts probably would not have been initiated.

Additional credibility is offered to this interpretation by noting also the essentially reactive nature of the more cooperative acts found to be defined by this first classificatory dimension. We would expect on theoretical grounds for nations to do things like request information, attempt to explain policy, surrender, or apologize in response to hostile foreign initiatives; these are the types of acts which it makes some sense to expect to co-occur with (hostile) warnings and accusations. If this reasoning is correct, therefore, then we may assume that factor I has defined for us rather adequately a descriptive category by which foreign policy acts of an essentially affective nature may be classified.

Our second factor is also amenable to rather compelling interpretation. We contend that it has isolated and defined for us a classificatory type describing participatory interaction activities between dyad partners, the kinds of acts states initiate toward one another in ordinary international discourse. It thus delineates a classificatory dimension containing the types of acts nations initiate routinely, without any affective connotation. We thus name this classificatory factor participation, and assume it describes activity and passivity in dyadic relationships. Since this type includes such foreign policy options as assurances, visitations and ceremonial greetings, we reason that it is describing the kind of activity nations normally engage in to perpetuate ongoing and established relations. These generally are of a peaceful nature, as we might expect them to be. Some support for this interpretation is offered by the observation that the variables loading highly on this factor include all those which the WEIS team has explicitly claimed and labeled to be of a participatory nature (McClelland and Hoggard, 1969: 714-715). Since these output variables thus seem to be of a dyadic-maintenance dimension of behavior, we will assume that we have correctly identified it as consisting of a participation type of foreign policy activity.

Before concluding our interpretation of the factors, one other observation might be offered to corroborate our diagnosis of the factors. As we noted previously, several of the variables were found to load rather highly on both dimensions. An examination of the substantive nature of these variables suggests this is reasonable, and reinforces rather than contradicts our prior interpretation. For instance, it would make sense to expect variables 4 and 12 (meet, agree to meet, respectively) to co-occur with behavior of either an affective or participatory nature; they would logically be a concomitant of either sort of dyadic relationship. The same would seem to apply to the other output options which load heavily on both categorical behavioral clusters: we would expect requests, commentary on situations, and yielding actions to be manifestations of either participatory or affective relations. Hence, the fact that these action variables are involved in both patterns makes sense. And it lends support to our contention that the interpretation we have given the factors is a realistic one.

Thus, these findings suggest that we have succeeded in our search for plausible dimensions with which types of foreign policy behavior may be differentiated. We have found two underlying and separate dimensions, which may be thought of as classificatory types (Rummel, 1970: 473-477), capable of dividing discrete kinds of foreign policy behavior into classes on the basis of their similarities and differences. The discovery of these polar dimensions therefore enables an empirical typology of foreign conduct to be built, one which can classify the types of foreign policy action states may direct toward each other in a parsimonious fashion.

This achievement does not end our mission, however. The discovery of typal dimensions is not regarded as an end in itself. We need to know further the classes of action which the dimensions define, as well as what behavior variables are subsumed under each class. This would yield our empirical typology. Moreover, as we have persistently argued, this empirical typology would be improved considerably if it could in addition show how the variables thus clustered relate to one another; by scaling, the resultant empirical typology would not only tell us the categories which most accurately classify the variables, but would also reveal to us how different are individual pairs of variables.

The circumplex model has the attractive feature of being able to accomplish both these goals. That is, a circumplex arrangement will define our empirical typology by placing the variables in terms of their similarity. We have already found some evidence, in our intercorrelation matrix of the variables, suggesting that such a circumplex configuration exists. What remains to be done is to probe this interrelationship among the variables more carefully, in order to discern the exact circumplicial pattern in its fullest detail.

The procedure for testing for the existence of a circular typological order of the external behavior variables is a rather straightforward one. At the risk of oversimplification, what this entails essentially is employing our discovered two categorical dimensions to construct a two-dimensional space on Cartesian coordinates. By treating these dimensions as coordinates, the vertical axis can then be allowed to represent the participation dimension while the horizontal axis appears as the affect dimension. The point of intersection of the two axes then represents neutrality on each dimension, and the circumplicial property-space is determined by rotating the radius (from the intersection or origin along any axis) 360° to define the circumference of a circle delineating the limits of the space. The taxonomical system is therefore formed because the categorical dimensions thus divide the circle into four quadrants representing four distinct classes of foreign policy behavior. To discern the existence and nature of a circumplex order for the variables, as well as to determine which variables fall under which of the resultant four categories, then involves, finally, plotting the factor loadings of the variables in this space and visually inspecting the order to see which class describes which variables and if the variables conform to the expected circular order (Kerlinger, 1964: 634-659; Cattell, 1950: 23-25).

To this end, the variables were plotted on the two coordinates according to their loadings on the two classificatory factors. Figure 4 portrays the arrangement of the variables schematically in this circumplicial space.

In order to enhance clarification of this order and to more clearly reveal the taxonomic structure as delineated by the obliquely rotated coordinates, the following additional diagram is provided (see Figure 5). This should serve as a visual aid in illustrating the relationships of the variables in the circumplex. This then allows us to formulate our empirical typology. As the results indicate, the quadrants define four distinct (mutually exclusive) classes or types of foreign policy behavior which

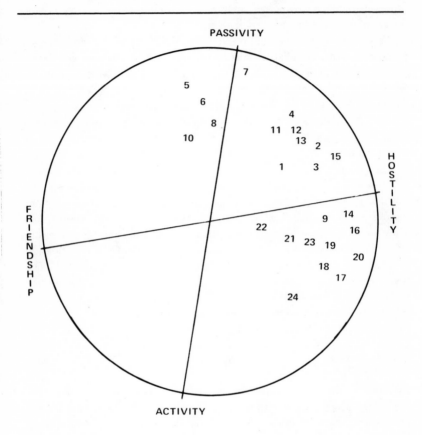

*Numbers refer to variable names given in correlation matrix, p. 35.

Figure 4: GRAPHICAL PORTRAYAL OF THE FOREIGN POLICY VARIABLES PLOTTED IN CIRCUMPLICIAL SPACE*

exhaustively categorize the 24 discrete kinds of action of our ad hoc typology. The constructed empirical typology is summarized for us in Table 8:

In examining the foregoing displays, several things about the arrangement and interrelationship of the variables in the typology now become vividly apparent. First, and perhaps most strikingly obvious, is the fact that our variables fail to satisfy—or even approximate—the defining characteristics of a perfectly ordered, uniform circumplex. Our data do not permit us to fit the variables into a uniform circumplex pattern. If

TABLE 8
Empirical Typology for Foreign Conduct

Empirical Categories	Active-Hostility	Passive-Hostility	Passive-Friendship	Active-Friendship
Discrete types of acts	Issue	Urge	Visit	
	Warning	Meet	Host	
	Charge	Comment	Promise	
	Protest	Request	Reward	
	Reject force	Agree to meet		
	Deny	Approve		
	Offer	Substantive		
	Expel-seize	Agreement		
	Grant	Explain		
	Threatening display	Yield		
	Reduce Relationship			

they had, the variables would have been arranged throughout the circle, equally spaced from one another and filling every quadrant (Guttman, 1954: 279). But such an aesthetically satisfying structure of the variables as that found in a perfect circumplex could not be found. Empirical reality simply did not possess such ordered features; only an approximate quasi-circumplex could be generated.

Secondly, and related to the above point, we note that the tendency toward a circular order of the variables is most upset by the existence of a rather wide gap in the typology: almost no variables appear on the side of friendship. We find no variables serving to define the "active-friendship" category, and but just a handful load in such a way as to provide us with a notion of the kinds of acts which are of a "passive-friendship" nature. This gap, however, need not disturb us. Very commonly circumplicial taxonomy studies are reported with rather large gaps showing a severe underrepresentation of variables relating to specific types delineated in the research effort (Carson, 1969: 103-106; Foa, 1961: 343-344). The presence of this gap does provide us with important information, however. Generally, we may interpret it as indicating to us on empirical grounds that none of the 24 action categories are adequately reflecting active-friendly behavior, and that new classificatory variables descriptive of that behavior might be profitably added. That is, our empirical typology suggests that the ad hoc WEIS category scheme may be biased against an adequate representation of friendly forms of behavior. It does not seem, on the basis of this evidence, to be sufficiently including coding categories

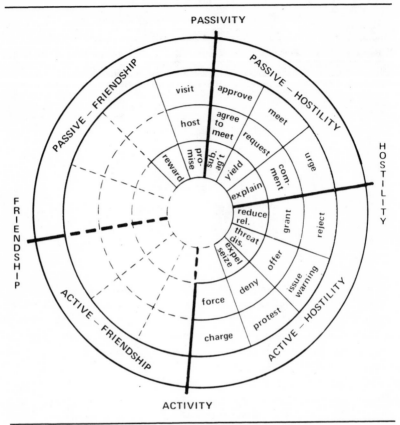

Figure 5: DIAGRAMATIC REPRESENTATION OF THE FOREIGN POLICY
OUTPUT CIRCUMPLEX STRUCTURE

which catch or reflect this type of behavior. But we should not push this interpretation too far, particularly in an exploratory study. Nevertheless, the finding does warrant further investigation. "Empirical typologies can," as Winch (1947: 75) has argued, "correct errors in heuristic typologies [and] can reveal types where none has been posited or suggested." The possible need for additional categories in the WEIS system suggested by this study would thus seem to deserve careful future attention.

With this aside in mind, we can also note, thirdly, that the circumplicial ordering of the variables arrived at above through mere inspection of the correlation matrix was indeed a rather crude one. Although suggestive, the order was not confirmable by the results obtained through plotting the loadings of the variables. The inconsistency of the results achieved through the two procedures is probably attributable to the unwillingness of the coefficients in the correlation matrix to conform to a uniform or easily interpretable perfect circumplex order, as well as to the inadequacy of visual inspection to precisely determine the most meaningful order or the variables on the basis of the patterns of intercorrelation. The structure arrived at through factor analytic investigation revealed the order to be much more complex and multifaceted than was discernible through mere perusal of the correlation matrix, for the cluster patterns existing in a large correlation matrix are not readily discoverable with the naked eye. Because any set of correlations can be variously interpreted, analysis on this basis tends to be unreliable. Hence we must give considerably more weight to the order of the variables revealed by the factor analytic solution.

The above observations about the nature of the results generated through factor analysis need not be a source of lament, however. Neither the disconfirmation of our hypothesis about an emergent perfect circumplex, nor the inability of the circular variable order derived from correlational techniques to hold up, should tarnish the significance of the quasi-circumplex typology that was achieved. Our intuitive hunches about the way the variables might be related is little more than conjectural hypothesizing; it should not be upsetting to discover that they are mistaken. And Guttman (1954: 287, 338) himself was careful to warn that "empirical examples . . . should not be expected to conform too closely to the . . . circumplex hypothesis." He went on to predict that only gross approximations could be anticipated with real data, and that deviations from a perfect circumplicial ordering need not lessen the importance of discovering an approximate one.

Hence it may be posited that although only a quasi-ordered circumplex for foreign policy behavior was found, one that only begins to resemble a perfect uniform circumplex, this is nevertheless a meaningful achievement. The utility of our finding a quasi-circular arrangement of international behavior has not been diminished because our circumplicial order still retains all of the essential properties of a circumplex which render it so attractive for typological purposes. That is, the main features of a uniform circumplex have been preserved and are intrinsic to our circumplex. Our version obeys the same law of sequential neighboring among variables having maximum dissimilarity. The variables thus adhere to the contiguity principle: they possess an order among themselves within the circular continuum, with each variable juxtapositioned in a fixed relationship to all others according to its relative resemblance to each of them. Our pattern, although imperfect, still enables us to inspect the ordering and determine which types of action are similar to each other, and which are not. The most useful function of the circumplex procedure, indeed the major justification for employing it, has therefore been provided by our analysis.

Moreover, our derived model has been successful in generating an empirical typology. It has permitted us to develop categories with which discrete types of external conduct may be classified. Our procedure identified for us the two principal dimensions of our behavioral domain, and these factors were then employed to construct a property-space for the reduction of the variables to a smaller number of generic classes. These classes, determined by the relationship of the dimensions to each other and the variables with both, divided the variables into distinct (mutually exclusive) clusters of homogeneous variables. This defined the empirical typology, outlining on the basis of the interrelationship of the variables a parsimonious (four category) typological system for describing and classifying external action. (It established boundaries between categories so as to maximize the similarity within each class and minimize that between them.) But our procedure did more than simply provide four independent categories for classifying the variables; it also revealed to us an organizational order for the four classes by showing how they are related to one another. Hence we have arrived at not only a set of four empirically distinct classificatory concepts, but we also have obtained a description of the degree to which those concepts reflect associated or polar opposite forms of behavior. The empirical classificatory concepts themselves, as well as the variables they subsume, have therefore been ordered.

These rather compelling features of our results, it is submitted, suggest that a worthwhile general empirical typology of external conduct has been generated, providing a sound basis for the classification and analysis of internation behavior. It has met the essential requirements of a scientific typology we have enumerated in detail previously, and would thus seem to have potential for contributing to the advancement of empirical research in internation relations. Because our technique has produced a typology of the way the world of foreign conduct is ordered which is unique in its amenability to external prediction (Guttman, 1954; Leary, 1957), so that it is directly applicable to testing of hypotheses about the determinants and consequences of external behavior, it should facilitate systematic foreign policy research. But whether our typological scheme is indeed fecund in its capacity to aid in the discovery and empirical confirmation of theoretical propositions is itself an empirical question whose solution must await further investigation. On the face of it, however, because our typology is a scientific one, the prospects for it establishing its utility (Simon, 1969: 54-58) appear promising.

DISCUSSION: UTILITY OF THE TYPOLOGY FOR POSITIVE THEORY CONSTRUCTION

As has been suggested, the discovery of evidence for the existence of an empirical typology is not an exercise in theory construction (Argyle, 1957: 60). An empirically derived typology is a set of usable dimensions and categories for the description and classification of phenomena, rather than a number of explanatory generalizations. A typology's essential function, therefore, is to enter into the formation of the predictive sentences which are the building blocks of theory. Since typologies are tools to be employed in theory construction, they are not appropriately evaluated as right or wrong but rather as useful or not useful.

Given this reasoning, the question of the utility of our empirical typology can be approached from several directions. First, if the value of a typology lies in its applicability to hypothesis testing, it is necessary to ask if a general typology such as ours is useful for the development of all kinds of theoretical statements about components of international behavior. The commonsense response (Brody, 1972: 47) to this query is that a general typology of foreign policy output is not equally relevant to the construction of all types of theory; general typologies are not general in the sense that they are applicable to all theories, but rather they are general in that they seek to delineate the fundamental dimensions by which the foreign policies of all cases (national actors) in the international system might be classified. All typologies serve to define boundaries within which conclusions may be regarded as applicable (Wood. 1969: 238), and a general typology of foreign policy output, by isolating the basic dimensions by which the external conduct of all states, irrespective of national characteristics, may be differentiated, is therefore applicable only to studies seeking to examine general patterns of interstate behavior. It follows, then, that general empirical typologies are most useful in the development of general positive theories of foreign policy. Such theories seek to develop as general descriptive or explanatory statements about external behavior as possible; a general theory "has as great an organizing power as possible so that it can encompass as many aspects of foreign policy behavior as possible" (McGowan, 1971: 1). The utility of a general typology is maximized when it is employed to develop such scientific generalizations and theories about the regularities of state behavior, but minimized in efforts to employ it to describe a particular country's policy in idiographic detail. The high generality of the typology means that the adequacy of the constructed categories in accounting for specific variations of particular cases is reduced. General typologies are not general purpose; they are of greatest utility in the development of general theories of foreign policy conduct.

A second aspect of the derived typology concerns its catholicity. A general typology purporting to provide a standard set of categories for the systematic description and classification of foreign policy acts must, if it is to be useful in future research, be universally valid. The derived typology must not be specific to the data analyzed in its construction or dependent on the statistical techniques employed; moreover, a general typology must be reliable over time and not unique to the population of cases (in this study, dyads) examined in its construction. Demonstrating the plausibility of an empirical typology through rigorous verification is not a simple process (Campbell and Fiske, 1959). However, elsewhere (Kegley, 1971: 305-354) a rather extensive validity check on the typology was conducted, which indicated that the resultant taxonomic structure was not specific to how time was treated between 1966 and 1969 and not unique to the actors and sample population of dyads included in the analysis. In addition, evidence for the ability of the structure to lead to external predictions (predictive validation) was found. The discovery of a typo-logical structure of national external behavior that is stable across time and population and capable of entering, to some extent, in scientific predictions, should augment our confidence in the findings.

The credibility of the structure would be enhanced further if there existed other independent typological studies of foreign policy behavior with which our results could be compared; unfortunately, no other typological studies exist which employ the directed dyad as the unit-of-analysis. However, it is interesting to note that the results presented here do not differ drastically from other typological works of foreign policy (McClelland and Hoggard, 1969; Salmore and Munton, 1973; Young, 1970; McGowan, 1972) which utilized a monadic conception of foreign policy in analysis. The convergence of our findings with these previous efforts, and the ability of all typological studies of external behavior to isolate very similar basic types of foreign policy behavior on the same or nearly identical fundamental dimensions, suggests that international behavior is very highly patterned and that the attempt to reveal the precise nature of that pattern through typal analysis is feasible and can be rewarding.

The high level of agreement on the nature and number of independent dimensions of foreign policy behavior in the international system is auspicious for the prospects of general positive theory development in foreign policy analysis. However, despite the existence of partial evidence for the generality and validity of the findings reported here, we should be cautious about accepting this typological delineation of the basic patterns of national external conduct as authoritative. Additional testing of the reliability and validity of the empirical typology is in order for confirmation of the findings. In short, acceptance of the typology requires additional replication efforts for verification, both in terms of application of the circumplex model to diverse data sets and in terms of efforts to reproduce the results through the application of other statistical data reduction procedures.

In assessing the circumplicial ordering of external behavior reported here, cognizance should be taken of a third use of empirical typologies in the development of theory in foreign policy studies. This is an empirical typology's capacity to provide a factual base for the conceptualization of behavioral phenomena. The categorization of external conduct derived by our analysis, by empirically delineating the major dimensions of foreign policy behavior, heuristically suggests the aspects of national external conduct which are most amenable to empirical inquiry and theoretical explanation. That is, the typology serves as a guide to future research by indicating which of the many features of foreign policy behavior is most likely to be related to theoretically important characteristics. Since the typology provides a description of basic patterns of foreign activity, it suggests which of the many competing definitional conceptualizations of foreign policy is likely to produce the greatest theoretical payoff in systematic treatment. In this sense, empirical typologies help us to assess the utility of definitional typologies (see pp. 8-9, above) in pre-theoretical conceptualization (Wood, 1969: 236-239; McKinney, 1966: 36-42); the empirical typology constructed here, as well as previous taxonomic efforts, indicates that the most theoretically advantageous dimensions with which to describe and classify interstate behavior is in terms of foreign policy affect and participation. This is a nonsurprising but important finding, since it provides empirically grounded guidance as to how general foreign policy theory research might most profitably proceed.

A fourth and final function of empirical typologies relates to the role they perform in the generation of general positive foreign policy theory. In addition to the uses discussed above, three further contributions of empirical typologies to theory development can be identified. The first basic role relates to the methodology of scientific inquiry in theory generation. Positive foreign policy theory made a major advance when pioneers in the field recognized that the analysis of foreign policy must be comparative if it was to be scientific (Rosenau, 1971; McGowan, 1970, 1972). Since empirical method acknowledges that classification is logically prior to comparison (Kalleberg, 1966; Isaak, 1969: 72-74), it was soon realized that the advance of positive theory about foreign policy was contingent upon an adequate categorization of foreign policy output, the basic dependent variable in most systematic foreign policy research. Hence typological work is crucial to empirical (comparative) studies of foreign policy. McClelland (1972: 27) lucidly described this function of typologies in scientific construction of foreign policy theory when he noted that foreign policy analysis must

> be made comparative. . . . To do this, one must provide a taxonomy for the various types of external conduct. . . . The insight is simply that there exists different kinds of foreign policy output and that, for comparative purposes, it is essential to discover which linked domestic or intrapolity processes are associated regularly with which types of foreign policy outputs. A classification system for foreign policy outputs could be built from the study of the flow of acts directed abroad by the polity or, in other words, by international event analysis. Virtually no work on this taxonomy has been undertaken to date. Once types of foreign policy output are known, the foreign policy analyst can begin to trace back the linked process to their domestic origin and to establish explanations (i.e., build models and express theories) of foreign policy formulation.

It is precisely this "taxonomy of foreign policy outputs" of which McClelland speaks which we have sought to derive by empirical procedures, for the purposes he cites. Once the types of foreign policy behavior have been isolated and identified by empirical procedures, theory construction can commence by applying comparative (scientific) techniques to search for the determinants that explain these similarities and differences in types of foreign policy behavior. The experience of the social sciences suggests that the discovery of an empirical typology of national external conduct should enhance our capacity to find compelling explanations of both the external outputs of states and the consequences of those outputs (Guttman, 1954).

A second use of the circumplicial typology of foreign behavior in positive theory construction relates to the contribution it can make to the objective description of state behavior. Although mere description is not theory, accurate description of behavior must precede explanation of it (Leng and Singer, 1970: 1). By ordering the acts states initiate in a circumplex configuration, the fundamental pattern of interstate behavior is described and this description can be employed as a prediction of the kinds of behavior one nation can expect to receive from another (Brody, 1972: 46). Based on past behavior, therefore, the circumplicial taxonomy enables us to reduce the domain of interactive behavior to a manageable size, to systematize this behavior into a factorially valid category system, and to identify the principal dimensions of the behavior (Carson, 1969: 98). A functional category system for interactive behavior is thereby discovered. The utility of the structure for empirical description and measurement is rather compelling. Because the resultant set of interaction variables are arranged along a circular two-dimensional continuum, a systematic relationship among them provides criteria for discriminating between neighboring variables. This ordering means that we now have a useful way for summarizing interaction behavior graphically for each actor; i.e., the numerical frequency for each generic act of an actor can be calculated and plotted, so that a descriptive profile is obtained in circular graphic summary form. (For possible example, see Figure 6.)

Thus once a circumplicial typology has been empirically derived, it becomes possible to graphically portray and thereby identify an actor's

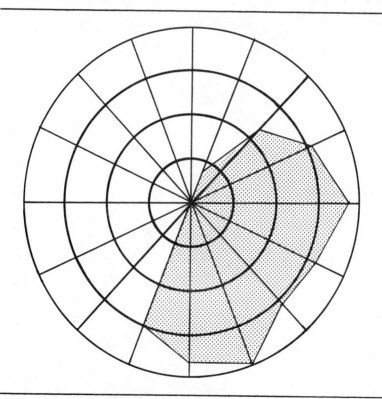

Figure 6: AN EXAMPLE OF HOW THE FOREIGN POLICY OF A STATE MAY BE SUMMARIZED GRAPHICALLY

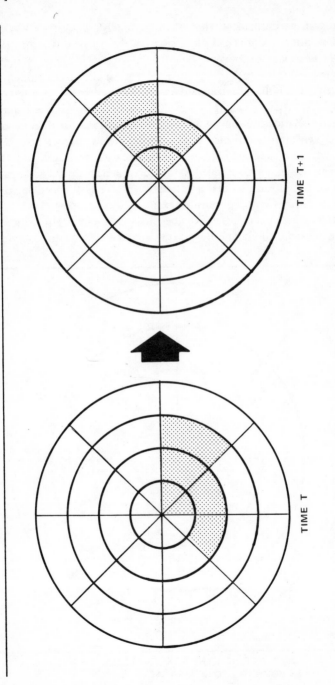

TIME T+1

TIME T

Figure 7: GRAPHIC REPRESENTATION OF BEHAVIORAL CHANGE

behavior in terms of its location in the circle. And, perhaps even more usefully, we will be able to classify the actor's behavior generically by converting the frequency of his acts into numerical indices which locate and define his foreign policy on the grid. That is, a summary point of the actor's behavior, placing him in a specific octant, can be determined mathematically (Leary, 1957: 68-69). This is possible because by considering the circle to be a two-dimensional array in ordinary Euclidian space, conventional trigometric and vector analytic formulas are able to weigh the magnitude of the components (discrete acts) in both directions and plot a summary point. Hence the circumplex ordering may serve as a device whereby the researcher may move from classification to index and scale construction (Guttman, 1954), i.e., to the quantitative measurement of foreign policy actions flowing between states in the international system.

The circumplex typological structure has the added feature of enabling a diachronic or longitudinal analysis of the change over time in an actor's behavior to be undertaken. This may be portrayed graphically, as in Figure 7. Or we may measure it diagramatically (see Figure 8).

Thus, the circumplicial typology permits us to study the behavior of an actor (1) at one time, through systematic pattern study of the structure of his behavior, and (2) temporally, by adding summaries of the same measurements as they change through time (Leary, 1957: 75).

A third and final but by no means exhaustive function of empirical typologies in the development of positive foreign policy theory is their capacity to aid in the formulation of if-then propositions. In the last analysis, typologies are justified by the theoretically important hypotheses they lead us to generate. A useful typology, therefore, should facilitate serendipitous discovery by provoking theoretical questions and suggesting hypotheses stating relationships between the typology and other variables that can be put to empirical scrutiny.

An estimation of the number of researchable propositions a typology is capable of generating depends upon the creativity and imagination of the individual investigator. The number of hypotheses a typology is able to enter into is indeterminate. Nevertheless, in order to illustrate the potential fruitfulness of our constructed typology for hypothesis generation, perhaps a few examples will suffice.

At perhaps the highest level of generality, it becomes possible to formulate an almost unlimited number of propositions for investigation regarding the determinants of a high incidence of the various types of external behavior identified by the typology. For instance, the categories of our typology may lead us to posit a relationship between national

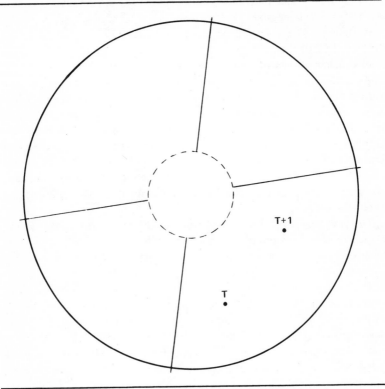

Figure 8: DIAGRAMMATIC REPRESENTATION OF BEHAVIOR CHANGE

attributes and foreign policy such as that "the less economically developed a state, the greater will be its tendency to manifest passive hostility in its foreign relations," or "the higher the political accountability of a society's governing elite, the greater will be its tendency to refrain from active-hostility in its foreign conduct." Moreover, systemic conditions may be postulated to covary with the frequency of certain kinds of external behavior, (e.g.: "active-hostility may be expected to increase between alliance partners under conditions of declining systemic bi-polarity"). Such propositions relating both national accounting variables and systemic variables to the behavior of states constitute the major emphasis in the contemporary comparative study of foreign policy field. A long neglected but theoretically important focus (Brody, 1972; Kegley, 1971; McGowan, 1972: 17) for future proposition building of this type pertains to the influence of dyadic attributes on the kind of behavior flowing between dyadic partners.

Our typology further is capable of heuristically suggesting a number of other kinds of propositions, at different levels of specificity, deserving of systematic empirical testing. For instance, the typology directs our attention to a cluster of dynamic narrow range propositions, which posit a relationship between past and future foreign policy behavior. These are of the form wherein the conduct of a nation at a given time is postulated to be determined by the nature of its previous behavior. Here our typology suggests propositions to the effect that "passive-hostility at time t is likely to be strongly correlated with active-hostility at time t+1;" or, "the greater the number of actively hostile acts a state received in any given period, the greater will be the number of actively-hostile acts it will initiate to others in the ensuing period."

Another form of proposition suggested by the typology is one which states relationships between the expected association of types of acts. The circumplex configuration directs our attention immediately to the propositions that "active and passive foreign policy hostility are strongly related," that "those who rank high on one type of behavior rank high on all types" (Brody, 1972: 55), and that "the more active a nation is in its external conduct, the more hostile that behavior will become." This suggestion that a nation's level of participation in the international system is related to the kind of behavior it manifests receives a good deal of empirical support in the literature. A variation of this sort of proposition would be to posit relationships between variables within the types themselves (e.g., "promises lead to visits") or to postulate necessary or sufficient conditions for types of behavior (e.g., "a state will not become actively-hostile toward another state without first issuing a warning to it") or for event sequences (e.g., "a precondition for reaching substantive foreign policy agreements is that both parties to the agreement reward and yield to each other").

A final exemplary sort of proposition suggested by the typology deals with the nature of behavior between interacting pairs of states, which would enable us to test various sociopsychological notions. For instance, the typology suggests the possibility of examining reciprocity and symmetry concepts of interstate interaction which posit that the kind of acts a state targets to another state resembles the kind of acts it will receive ("the hostility you take is equal to the hostility you make," to paraphrase the Beatles). The possibilities for forming hypotheses which link particular types of action with particular types of foreign policy response are great.

In sum, it is hoped that the foregoing discussion suggests that the derivation of a typology of foreign policy conduct by empirical procedures is a needed and useful endeavor in the development of general positive theories of external conduct. At a minimum, the present study should demonstrate that powerful classificatory techniques exist with which to isolate the basic types of complex phenomena. This finding should in and of itself comprise sufficient motivation to increase our efforts to validate the structure uncovered by this study, so that we may proceed with the generation of scientific theories of foreign policy behavior.

NOTES

1. That is, comprehension requires conceptualization. Before we can understand an object, our mind inevitably forms a cognitive abstraction or conceptualization of it, whereby the similarities and differences between the properties that comprise it are perceived. Hence, conceptualization or typology construction, the attempt to classify the attributes of an object along various dimensions, is endemic to all thinking and explanation, because in order to discuss objects people must inevitably form at least implicit categories and labels for the phenomena they observe.

2. The reader should note that the listing is only a nonexhaustive (but hopefully somewhat representative) sample of some of the ways in which the foreign postures of states have been classified; moreover, the reader should be warned that while the table has juxtaposed similar classifications next to each other for comparative purposes, the juxtaposition is not intended to suggest that scholars adopting similar descriptive categories have necessarily conceptualized those categories in the same way. Nor should the juxtaposition be taken to imply that the categories refer to exactly the same dimensions of foreign policy; they are only roughly similar approximations. The table is designed to merely provide a concise and heuristic literature review of some of the more common existing typologies of the behavior patterns of international actors.

3. Events/interactions are taken to mean, usually, the official governmental acts between states of a nonroutine and therefore newsworthy sort. They do not include as relevant the regularized flow of acts between nations that are continuous and undramatic (i.e., transactions such as foreign trade, book exchanges, or tourist travel); nor does it strive to categorize or collect data on internal events.

4. This is not to imply that we can ever know with certainty the empirical structure of reality. "No concept," McKinney (1966) argues, "is ever a copy of anything real . . . ; unreality is characteristic of all concepts." Yet the distortion can be minimized by scientific methods of typological construction. The statistical control of the scientific technique enables the researcher to estimate how plausible his discovered typology is; that is, he can determine the probability that the typology is a true reflection of empirical reality.

5. Meaningful classes may be said to have been discovered when the types identified are demonstrated in research to be "important as a cause of or an effect of other phenomena" (Stinchcombe: 1968: 45). Torgerson (1958: 24) concurs with this position when he argues that the value of a concept lies in its ability to enter into a large number of simple relations with other variables. Kaplan (1964: 50) makes the same point succinctly: "a significant concept so groups or divides its subject-matter

that it can enter into many important true propositions about the subject matter other than those which state the classification itself . . . such a concept is said to identify a 'natural' class rather than an 'artificial' one."

6. I wish to thank Professor Patrick J. McGowan for first drawing the literature of this taxonomic technique to my attention and suggesting its relevance to the study of foreign policy behavior.

7. This was the coefficient recommended by Guttman. Our data meet the assumptions of this coefficient, although it should be noted that it required transforming variables 17 and 24 into their own square root.

8. As Carson (1969: 97) describes such a graphical representation: "An arrangement of this kind would . . . therefore place . . . similar variables in proximity to each other around the circumference . . . and would give maximum sequential separation between variables having maximum . . . dissimilarity. In general, variables at either end of any diameter of such a circle would be maximally dissimilar (perhaps 'opposite') . . . whereas immediately adjacent variables, having relatively high inter-correlations, would be maximally similar." Unfortunately, a quasicircumplicial order cannot be displayed in this way meaningfully.

9. Placing the squared multiple correlations, rather than unities, in the principal diagonal as initial communality estimates was recommended because that procedure yields results which are descriptive only of that which is common (descriptive only of the variance a variable shares with another variable). Selecting multiple r^2 thus enables our factors to account for only shared variance, which is our primary aim. It is the more conservative option in that it does not require us to make assumptions about the nonpresence of specific variance and random error among the vectors.

10. The problem of deciding on the proper criteria to employ to determine the number of factors to extract is an important but vexatious one, and is usually reached on the (arbitrary) basis of the researcher's needs and judgment. The general principle that should be adhered to is that it is permissible to stop factoring when the last factor accounts for the most significant portion of the meaningful variance. Coomb's criterion seemed to determine this for us in a satisfactory and parsimonious fashion. It indicated to us that a bifactor solution was sufficient to account for most of the common variance. Interestingly enough, the eigenvalue for this potential third factor was only 1.1 which is close enough to the eigenvalue-one criterion to suggest that a third factor was indeed unwarranted.

11. It should also be noted that simple structure (oblique) rotation determines invariant factors (i.e., a unique factor solution is discoverable). This is further reason for employing this procedure, since it enhances the prospects for replication by rendering the patterns comparable from one study to another.

12. Although further analysis of the orthogonally rotated matrix will not be offered, the reader should examine it carefully because it defines the two classes of foreign action for us as if they were maximally dissimilar.

13. Additional research has been conducted to ascertain the validity of the results. These validity tests discovered that the resultant taxonomic structure was not specific to a particular span of history and not unique to the actors and sample population of dyads included in the analysis. And evidence for the ability of the structure to lead to external predictions (predictive validation) was found (see Kegley, 1971: 305-355).

14. The reader desirous of employing circumplicial typologies in his research should consult such works as Guttman, Carson, and Leary for descriptions of the appropriate methodologies to follow.

REFERENCES

ADELMAN, M. L. (1972) "Crisis decision-making and cognitive balance." Sage Professional Paper, International Studies Series 1: 61-94.

ARGYLE, M. (1957) The Scientific Study of Social Behavior. London: Methuen.

AZAR, E. E. (1970) "Analysis of international events." Peace Research Rev. 4 (November).

––– and M. RHODES (1970) "International events: a manual for coders." Michigan State University. (mimeo)

AZAR, E. E., S. H. COHEN, T. O. JUKAM, and J. McCORMICK (1972) "Making and measuring the international event as a unit of analysis." Sage Professional Paper, International Studies Series 1: 59-77.

BARTON, A. H. (1955) "The concept of property-space in social research," pp. 40-53 in P. F. Lazarsfeld and M. Rosenberg (eds.) The Language of Social Research. New York: Free Press.

BRODY, R. A. (1972) "International events: problems of measurement and analysis." Sage Professional Paper, International Studies Series 1: 45-58.

BURGESS, P. M. (1970) "Nation-typing for foreign policy analysis: a partitioning procedure for constructing typologies," pp. 1-50 in E. H. Fedder (ed.) Methodological Concerns in International Studies. St. Louis: University of Missouri.

CAMPBELL, D. T. and D. W. FISKE (1959) "Convergent and discriminant validation by the multi-trait-multimethod." Psych. Bull. 56 (March): 81-105.

CARSON, R. C. (1969) Interaction Concepts of Personality. Chicago: Aldine.

CATTELL, R. B. (1950) Personality: A Systematic, Theoretical, and Factual Study. New York: McGraw-Hill.

CICOUREL, A. V. (1964) Method and Measurement in Sociology. New York: Free Press.

COPLIN, W. D. (1971) Introduction to International Politics: A Theoretical Overview. Chicago: Markham.

DEUTSCH, K. W. (1963) "The limits of common sense," pp. 51-58 in N. W. Polsby, R. A. Dentler, and P. A. Smith (eds.) Politics and Social Life. Boston: Houghton Mifflin.

––– S. BURRELL, R. KANN, M. LEE, M. LICHTERMAN, R. LINDGREN, F. LOEWENHEIM, and R. VAN WAGENEN (1957) Political Community in the North Atlantic Area. Princeton, N.J.: Princeton Univ. Press.

DIXON, W. J. [ed.] (1969) BMD Biomedical Computer Programs, X-series Supplement: University of California Publications in Automatic Computation, No. 3. Berkley: Univ. of California Press.

––– [ed.] (1968) BMD Biomedical Computer Programs: University of California Publications in Automatic Computation, No. 22. Berkley: Univ. of California Press.

DUVERGER, M. (1964) An Introduction to the Social Sciences. (Malcolm Anderson, trans.) New York: Praeger.

ETZIONI, A. and E. W. LEHMAN (1969) "Some dangers in 'valid' social measurement," pp. 45-62 in B. M. Gross (ed.) Social Intelligence for America's Future. Boston: Allyn & Bacon.

FIELD, J. O. (1972) "The Sino-Indian border conflict: an exploratory analysis of action and perception." Sage Professional Paper, International Studies Series 1: 31-59.

FOA, U. G. (1961) "Convergences in the analysis of the structure of interpersonal behavior." Psych. Rev. 68: 341-353.

——— (1958) "The contiguity principle in the structure of interpersonal relations." Human Relations 11: 229-238.

GARDNER, R. W. (1953) "Cognitive styles in categorizing behavior." J. of Personality 22: 214-233.

GARSON, G. D. (1971) Handbook of Political Science Methods. Boston: Holbrook.

GOODE, W. J. and P. K. HATT (1958) Methods in Social Research. New York: McGraw-Hill.

GUTTMAN, L. (1954) "A new approach to factor analysis: the radex," pp. 258-348 in P. F. Lazarsfeld (ed.) Mathematical Thinking in the Social Sciences. New York: Free Press.

HEMPEL, C. G. (1952) Fundamentals of Concept Formation in Empirical Science. Chicago: Univ. of Chicago Press.

HERMANN, C. F. (1972) "Policy classification: a key to the comparative study of foreign policy," pp. 58-79 in Rosenau, J. N., V. Davis, and M. A. East (eds.) The Analysis of International Politics. New York: Free Press.

——— (1971) "What is a foreign policy even?" pp. 295-321 in W. F. Hanrieder (ed.) Comparative Foreign Policy: Theoretical Essays. New York: McKay.

HILL, G. A. (1971) "The flow of international events: July-December, 1970." University of Southern California. (mimeo)

HOLSTI, K. J. (1967) International Politics: A Framework for Analysis. Englewood Cliffs, N.J.: Prentice-Hall.

HOLSTI, O. R., R. A. BRODY, and R. C. NORTH (1968) "Perception and action in the 1914 crisis," pp. 123-158 in J. D. Singer (ed.) Quantitative International Politics. New York: Free Press.

ISAAK, A. C. (1969) Scope and Methods of Political Science. Homewood, Ill.: Dorsey.

KALLEBERG, A. L. (1966) "The logic of comparison: a methodological note on the comparative study of political systems." World Politics 19 (October): 69-82.

KAPLAN, A. (1964) The Conduct of Inquiry. San Francisco: Chandler.

KEGLEY, C. W., Jr. (1972a) "Applying events data to the measurement of systemic transformation: problems and prospects." Presented at the International Studies Association South Meeting of the Southern Political Science Association, Atlanta, November.

——— (1972b) "The pattern of foreign policy interactions in Asia: a quantitative comparison." Presented at the Annual Meeting of the Association for Asian Studies, Salt Lake City, November.

——— (1971) "Toward the construction of an empirically grounded typology of foreign policy output behavior." Ph.D. dissertation. Syracuse University.

KERLINGER, F. N. (1964) Foundations of Behavioral Research. New York: Holt, Rinehart & Winston.

KRETSCHMER, S. (1925) Physique and Character. New York: Harcourt, Brace & World.

KRIEGER, A. D. (1944) "The typological concept." Amer. Antiquity 9 (January): 271-288.

KUHN, T. S. (1962) The Structure of Scientific Revolutions. Chicago: Univ. of Chicago Press.

KULSKI, W. W. (1968) International Politics in A Revolutionary Age. Philadelphia: Lippincott.

LaFORGE, R. and R. SUCZEK (1957) "The interpersonal adjective checklist," pp. 458-467 in T. F. Leary, Interpersonal Diagnosis of Personality. New York: Ronald.

LANDAU, M. (1972) Political Theory and Political Science. New York: Macmillan.

LAZARSFELD, P. F. (1962) "Philosophy of science and empirical social research," pp. 463-473 in E. Nagel, P. Suppes, and A. Takski (eds.) Logic, Methodology and Philosophy of Science. Stanford: Stanford Univ. Press.

——— (1937) "Some remarks on the typological procedures in social research." Zeitschrift für Socialforschung 6: 119-139.

——— and N. W. HENRY (1968) Latent Structure Analysis. Boston: Houghton Mifflin.

LAZARSFELD, P. F. and A. H. BARTON (1955) "Some general principles of questionnaire classification," pp. 83-92 in P. F. Lazarsfeld and M. Rosenberg (eds.) The Language of Social Research. New York: Free Press.

——— (1951) "Qualitative measurement in the social sciences: classification, typologies and indices," pp. 155-192 in D. Lerner and H. D. Lasswell (eds.) The Policy Sciences. Stanford: Stanford Univ. Press.

LEARY, T. F. (1957) Interpersonal Diagnosis of Personality. New York: Ronald.

LENG, R. J. and J. D. SINGER (1970) "Toward a multi-theoretical typology of international behavior." (mimeo)

LERCHE, C. O., Jr. and A. SAID (1963) Concepts of International Politics. Englewood Cliffs, N.J.: Prentice-Hall.

LONDON, K. (1965) The Permanent Crisis. Waltham, Mass.: Blaisdell.

——— (1965) The Making of Foreign Policy. Philadelphia: J. B. Lippincott.

LORR, M. and D. McNAIR (1965) "Expansion of the interpersonal behavior circle." J. of Personality and Social Psychology 2: 823-830.

McCLELLAND, C. A. (1972) "Some effects on theory from the international event analysis movement." Sage Professional Paper, International Studies Series 1: 15-44.

——— (1970) "Two conceptual issues in the quantitative analysis of international event data." University of Southern California. (mimeo)

——— (1969) "International Interaction analysis in the predictive mode." University of Southern California. (mimeo)

——— (1968a) "Access to Berlin: the quantity and variety of events, 1948-1963," pp. 159-187 in J. D. Singer (ed.) Quantitative International Politics. New York: Free Press.

——— (1968b) "International interaction analysis: basic research and some practical applications, World Event/Interaction Survey Technical Depart 2. University of Southern California. (mimeo)

——— (1967) "The World Event/Interaction Survey: a research project on theory and measurement of international interaction and transaction." University of Southern California. (mimeo)

——— and A. ANCOLI (1970) "An interaction survey of the Middle East." University of Southern California. (mimeo)

McCLELLAND, C. A. and G. D. HOGGARD (1969) "Conflict patterns in the interactions among nations," pp. 711-724 in J. N. Rosenau (ed.) International Politics and Foreign Policy. New York: Free Press.

McGOWAN, P. J. (1972) "Dimensions of African foreign policy behavior." Presented at the Annual Meeting of the Canadian Association of African Studies, Ottawa, February.

——— (1973) "Problems in the construction of positive foreign policy theory," in J. N. Rosenau (ed.) Comparing Foreign Policy. Beverly Hills: Sage Pubns.

——— (1970) "Theoretical approaches to the comparative study of foreign policy." Ph.D. dissertation. Northwestern University.

McKINNEY, J. C. (1966) Constructive Typology and Social Theory. New York: Appleton-Century-Crofts.

MADGE, J. (1965) The Tools of Social Science. New York: Doubleday-Anchor.

MADRON, T. M. (1969) Small Group Methods and the Study of Politics. Evanston: Northwestern.

MEEHAN, E. J. (1968) Explanation in Social Science: A System Paradigm. Homewood, Ill.: Dorsey.

MISCHEL, W. (1968) Personality and Assessment. New York: Wiley.

MODELSKI, G. A. (1962) A Theory of Foreign Policy. New York: Praeger.

MORGENTHAU, H. J. (1967) Politics Among Nations. New York: Alfred A. Knopf.

MORSE, E. L. (1970) "The transformation of foreign policies." World Politics 22 (April): 371-392.

ORGANSKI, A.F.K. (1968) World Politics. New York: Alfred A. Knopf.

PUCHALA, D. J. (1969a) "Charles DeGaulle as an independent variable?" Presented at the American Political Science Association Convention, New York, September.

——— (1969b) "Recording West European diplomatic interaction." Presented at the American Political Science Association Convention, New York, September.

ROSENAU, J. N. (1971) The Scientific Study of Foreign Policy. New York: Free Press.

——— (1969a) "Intervention as a scientific concept." J. of Conflict Resolution 13 (June): 149-171.

——— (1969b) "Introduction: political science in a shrinking world," pp. 1-20 in Linkage Politics. New York: Free Press.

——— and G. D. HOGGARD (1971) "Foreign policy behavior in dyadic relationships; testing a pre-theoretical extension." Presented at the Annual Meeting of the International Studies Association, San Juan, Puerto Rico, March.

RUDNER, R. S. (1966) Philosophy of Sicence. Englewood Cliffs, N.J.: Prentice-Hall.

RUMMEL, R. J. (1970) Applied Factor Analysis. Evanston, Ill.: Northwestern Univ. Press.

——— (1969) "Some dimensions in the foreign behavior of nations," pp. 600-621 in J. N. Rosenau (ed.) International Politics and Foreign Policy. New York: Free Press.

——— (1967) "Understanding factor analysis." J. of Conflict Resolution 11 (December): 444-480.

——— (1963) "Dimensions of conflict behavior within and between nations." General Systems Yearbook 8: 1-50.

RUNCIMAN, W. G. (1965) Social Science and Political Theory. Cambridge: Cambridge Univ. Press.

SALMORE, S. A. and D. MUNTON (1973) "Classifying foreign policy behaviors: an empirically based typology," in J. N. Rosenau (ed.) Comparing Foreign Policy. Beverly Hills: Sage Pubns.

SALMORE, S. A. and B. G. SALMORE (1970) "National attributes and foreign policy: the role of political accountability." Presented at the Annaul Meeting of the American Political Science Association, Los Angeles, September.

SCHAEFFER, E. S. (1959) "A circumplex model for maternal behavior." J. of Abnormal and Social Psychology 59 (September): 226-235.

SEDERBERG, P. C. (1972) "Subjectivity and typification: a note on method in the social sciences." Philosophy of Social Science 2: 167-176.

SELVIN, H. C. and W. O. HAGSTROM (1963) "The empirical classification of groups." Amer. Soc. Rev. 28 (June): 399-411.

SIGLER, J. H. (1972) "Reliability problems in the measurement of international events in the elite press." Sage Professional Paper, International Studies Series 1: 9-29.

SIMON, J. L. (1969) Basic Research Methods in Social Science: The Art of Empirical Investigation. New York: Random House.

SJOBERG, G. (1970) "The comparative method in the social sciences," pp. 25-38 in A. Etzioni and F. L. Dubow (eds.) Comparative Perspectives. Boston: Little, Brown.

SOKAL, R. R. and P.H.A. SNEATH (1963) Principles of Numerical Taxonomy. San Francisco: Freeman.

STINCHCOMBE, A. L. (1968) Constructing Social Theories. New York: Harcourt, Brace & World.

SULLIVAN, D. G. (1963) "Towards an inventory of major propositions contained in contemporary textbooks in international relations." Ph.D. dissertation. Northwestern University.

TORGERSON, W. S. (1958) Theory and Methods of Scaling. New York: Wiley.

VAN DYKE, V. (1966) International Politics. New York: Appleton-Century-Crofts.

VINCENT, J. C. (1969) "Factor analysis as a research tool in international relations." Presented at the Annual Meeting of the American Political Science Association, New York, September.

WILKINSON, D. O. (1969) Comparative Foreign Relations. Belmont, Calif.: Dickenson.

WINCH, R. F. (1947) "Heuristic and empirical typologies: a job for factor analysis." Amer. Soc. Rev. 12 (February): 68-75.

WOLFERS, A. (1962) Discord and Collaboration. Baltimore: Johns Hopkins Univ. Press.

WOOD, A. L. (1969) "Ideal and empirical typologies for research in deviance and control." Sociology and Social Research 53 (January): 227-241.

YOUNG, R. A. (1970) "A classification of nations according to foreign policy output." Presented at the Annual Meeting of the American Political Science Association, Los Angeles, September.

――― and W. R. MARTIN (1968) "A review of six international event/interaction category and scaling methods." University of Southern California. (mimeo)

APPENDIX A
A Rank Order of 91 National Foreign Policy Actors in Terms of the Number of Nations to Which They Directed Five or More Acts

Actor[a]	No. of Targets (Dyads)	Freq. (Σ)	Mean No. of Acts Per Target	Standard Deviation
USA	70	2207	31.5	50.8
USR	34	1359	39.9	75.8
CHN	23	721	31.3	53.1
UNK	23	475	20.6	21.0
VTN	12	1304	108.7	240.0
GMW	12	317	26.4	31.4
ISR	11	645	58.6	75.9
UAR	11	496	45.1	65.2
FRN	11	295	26.8	30.9
SYR	10	190	19.0	21.7
CZE	9	204	22.7	31.3
TUR	9	93	10.3	6.2
IND	8	198	24.8	22.5
IRQ	8	78	9.6	4.2
JOR	7	279	39.9	68.0
GME	7	158	22.6	25.8
POL	7	103	14.7	11.4
YUG	7	94	13.4	9.9
INS	7	93	13.3	9.2
RUM	6	80	13.3	8.6
ALG	6	58	9.6	4.8
JAP	5	132	26.4	31.1
CAN	5	107	21.4	18.3
CUB	5	90	18.0	20.1
PAK	5	89	17.8	14.9
CAM	4	133	33.3	44.0
ITA	4	55	13.6	9.2
NIG	4	55	13.6	4.2
MAL	4	43	10.6	8.9
POR	4	24	6.0	1.4
VTS	3	162	54.0	50.1
KON	3	139	46.3	35.5
KOS	3	130	43.3	32.3
NIG	3	102	34.0	40.1
PHI	3	67	22.3	12.1
LAO	3	49	16.3	15.5
GRC	3	47	15.7	8.6
AUL	3	46	15.3	16.2
TAI	3	39	13.0	13.0
BEL	3	37	12.3	7.0
HUN	3	36	12.0	4.0
LEB	3	30	10.0	6.1
ALB	3	28	9.3	3.5

APPENDIX A (Continued)

GHA	3	25	8.3	0.6
NEW	3	25	8.3	1.5
BUL	3	22	7.3	2.3
SUD	3	17	5.6	0.6
SPN	2	47	23.5	24.7
SWD	2	39	19.5	14.8
BRA	2	29	14.5	7.8
SAU	2	29	14.5	9.2
MON	2	28	14.0	2.8
SAF	2	23	11.5	4.9
IRN	2	22	11.0	7.1
ZAM	2	20	10.0	4.2
YEM	2	19	9.5	4.9
SIN	2	19	9.5	0.7
COP	2	17	8.5	4.9
NTH	2	17	8.5	0.7
CYP	2	15	7.5	0.7
TAZ	2	14	7.0	0.0
AUS	2	14	7.0	2.8
NOR	2	12	6.0	1.4
GUY	2	12	6.0	0.0
BUR	2	11	5.5	0.5
URU	2	11	5.5	0.7
VEN	2	10	5.0	0.0
PER	1	31	31.0	—
MEX	1	17	17.0	—
ELS	1	17	17.0	—
ECU	1	17	17.0	—
HON	1	16	16.0	—
ARG	1	16	16.0	—
COL	1	15	15.0	—
IRE	1	13	13.0	—
FIN	1	12	12.0	—
RHO	1	11	11.0	—
CHL	1	11	11.0	—
DEN	1	9	9.0	—
TUN	1	9	9.0	—
GUI	1	9	9.0	—
PAN	1	9	9.0	—
CHT	1	8	8.0	—
ETH	1	7	7.0	—
KUW	1	7	7.0	—
BOL	1	7	7.0	—
SWZ	1	6	6.0	—
MOR	1	5	5.0	—
DOM	1	5	5.0	—
HAI	1	5	5.0	—
GUA	1	5	5.0	—

a. See Kegley (1971: 177-178) for a table of actor abbreviations.

APPENDIX B

Sample Population of 452 Dyads Classified According to Dyadic Genotype

Dyad Type	Dyads						n	% of Sample Dyads (453)	No. Acts	Mean No. Acts Per Dyad	Std. Dev.
Remote-Similar-Equal	GMW-USA FRN-USA USA-GMW	USA-GMW USA-FRN PAK-IRN	USA-UNK CUB-SPN USR-CHN	CHN-USR PAK-IRN			11	.03	917	86.4	19.2
Remote-Similar-Unequal	ISR-GMW AUL-FRN ISR-FRN USA-ITA CAN-FRN AUL-UNK CAN-UNK	GMW-CAN FRN-CAN UNK-CAN CHN-CZE RUM-CHN ALB-CHN CZE-CHN POL-CHN	NEW-USA AUL-USA ISR-USA DEN-USA NOR-USA SWD-USA GRC-USA ITA-USA	AUS-USA SWZ-USA BEL-USA CHN-ALB CHN-YUG USR-VTN USR-KON NTH-USA	USA-AUL VTN-USR KON-USR USA-SWZ USA-GRC USA-NTH USA-BEL UNK-AUL	USA-ISR UNK-ISR FRN-ISR GMW-ISR USA-NOR USA-SWD CHN-RUM	47	.10	729	15.5	16.2
Remote-Dissimilar-Equal	VTN-CAN CHN-USA USR-USA	CHN-FRN CHN-UNK CHN-GMW	USA-USR VTN-SWD GMW-CHN	UNK-CHN USA-CHN YUG-UAR	IND-UAR CUB-VTN IND-YUG	UAR-YUG	16	.04	1170	73.1	131.0
Remote-Dissimilar-Unequal	USA-JAP USR-JAP CHN-ITA SYR-FRN UAR-FRN VTS-FRN VTN-FRN LAO-FRN ALG-FRN UNK-INS JOR-UNK SYR-UNK UAR-UNK IRQ-UNK	SUD-UNK ALG-UNK SAF-UNK RHO-UNK ZAM-UNK TAZ-UNK VTN-UNK IND-UNK NIG-UNK GHA-UNK GME-UNK POR-USA SPN-USA ALB-USA	CZE-USA HUN-USA POL-USA GHA-USA GUI-USA RUM-USA BUL-USA YUG-USA CHN-CAN USR-CAN INS-USA PHI-USA MAL-USA VTS-USA	VTN-USA LAO-USA CAM-USA TAI-USA PAK-USA IND-USA JAP-USA KOS-USA KON-USA CHI-USA KUW-USA YEM-USA SAU-USA JOR-USA	LEB-USA SYR-USA UAR-USA IRQ-USA IRN-USA SUD-USA TUN-USA ALG-USA MOR-USA SAF-USA ETH-USA TAZ-USA COP-USA	NIG-USA CAN-USR CUB-USR BRA-USR GHA-USR NIG-USR KEN-USR ALG-USR IRQ-USR UAR-USR SYR-USR JOR-USR ISR-USR JAP-USr	168	.37	3727	22.1	34.7
Proximate-Dissimilar-Equal	CHN-MON USR-FRN USR-UNK INS-JAP KOS-JAP GMW-USR FRN-USR	UNK-USR ALG-ISR TUR-GRC SYR-ISR UAR-ISR IRO-ISR BUR-IND	PAK-IND GRC-TUR JAP-INS IND-PAK AUL-MAL PHI-MAL TAI-MAL	RHO-ZAM INS-PHI MAL-PHI ZAM-RHO VTN-VTS PHI-VTS AUL-VTS TAI-VTS	ISR-IRQ GHA-GUI IND-BUL VTN-VTS PHI-VTS AUL-VTS TAI-VTS	VTS-VTN KOS-KON MAL-TAI SUD-ETH KOS-TAI JAP-KOS KON-KOS	42	.09	1441	34.31	47.3

APPENDIX B (Continued)

Category					
Proximate-Dissimilar-Unequal	83	.18	1553	18.71	30.9
Proximate-Similar-Equal	43	.09	671	15.6	13.
Proximate-Similar-Unequal	42	.09	799	19.0	28.

Proximate-Dissimilar-Unequal

URU-USA	HAI-USA	POR-GMW	TUR-CYP	USA-BRA	USA-DOM
ARG-USA	CUB-USA	UNK-SPN	USR-AUS	USA-TUR	USA-ECU
CHL-USA	USR-ITA	FRN-POL	USA-PAN	CYP-TUR	USA-PER
BOL-USA	USA-MEX	GMW-POL	GUY-VEN	CHN-INS	USA-BOL
BRA-USA	USA-ARG	NOR-USR	USA-CHL	CHN-PAK	CAM-VTS
PER-USA	CHN-JAP	SWD-USR	JOR-ISR	INS-CHN	LAO-VTN
ECU-USA	SPN-UNK	FIN-USR	LEB-ISR	BUR-CHN	VTN-LAO
GUY-USA	FIN-USR	ITA-USR	USA-CUB	PAK-CHN	VTN-CAM
VEN-USA	ITA-USR	AUS-USR	GMW-GME	IND-CHN	CHN-CAM
COL-USA	AUS-USR	SPN-USR	FRN-GME	JAP-CHN	ISR-JOR
PAN-USA	SPN-USR	BEL-USR	GMW-POR	CHI-CHN	GMW-POR
GUA-USA	BEL-USR	TUR-USR	GMW-RUM	ISR-LEB	GMW-YUG
MEX-USA	CZE-GMW	USA-FIN	FRN-RUM	USA-ELS	CHN-BUL
DOM-USA	POL-GMW	USA-SWD	CHN-IND	USA-COL	
	GME-GMW				

Remote-Dissimilar-Unequal (con'd)

IND-USR	USR-BUL	USR-MAL	FRN-ETH	USA-IRQ	FRN-VTN
PAK-USR	USR-BRA	USA-TUN	USA-GUI	UNK-IRQ	USA-VTS
MAL-USR	USA-TUR	UNK-RHO	USA-GHA	USR-IRQ	UNK-VTS
USA-POL	USA-IND	USA-RHO	CHN-GHA	USA-UAR	OSA-LAO
USA-SPN	USR-IND	USA-MOR	USR-GHA	UNK-UAR	USA-CAM
COP-BEL	USA-PAK	POR-ZAM	USR-NIG	USR-UAR	USA-TAI
CHN-NTH	USR-PAK	UNK-ZAM	UNK-NIG	USR-SYR	USA-KOS
USR-ISR	TAZ-CHN	CHN-TAZ	USA-ALG	USA-JOR	USA-KON
USA-SAF	GHA-CHN	USA-COP	FRN-ALG	UNK-JOR	USA-CHI
USR-CUB	BEL-CHN	BEL-COP	USR-ALG	USR-JOR	UNK-YEM
USA-CZE	NTH-CHN	USR-COP	USA-NIG	ZAM-POR	USA-YEM
USA-HUN	USR-INS	ALG-COP	USA-SUD	USA-POR	USA-SAU
USA-RUM	USA-INS	USA-YUG	USA-IRN	USA-VTN	USR-YEM
USA-GME	USA-PHI	USA-ETH	USR-IRN	UNK-VTN	

Proximate-Similar-Equal

GMW-FRN	ORC-DEN	HUN-CZE	ALG-MOR	UAR-SAU	SYR-ALG
UNK-FRN	YUG-RUM	POL-CZE	ELS-HON	IRQ-IRN	RUM-YUG
GMW-UNK	CZE-RUM	RUM-CZE	HON-ELS	IRQ-UAR	CZE-YUG
FRN-UNK	YUG-BUL	BUL-CZE	UAR-SYR	ALG-UAR	
FRN-GMW	GME-RUM	CZE-HUN	IRQ-SYR	SYR-IRQ	
UNK-GMW	VEN-CUB	CZE-GME	SYR-UAR	UAR-IRQ	
CZE-POL	GME-CZE	MAL-INS	UAR-IRQ	KOS-VTS	
ITA-GRC	YUG-CZE	INS-MAL	SYR-SAU	MOR-ALG	

Proximate-Similar-Unequal

ITA-UNK	POL-USR	FIN-USR	USR-HUN	TUN-UAR	USR-JOR
GRC-UNK	GME-USR	GRC-CYP	USR-CZE	SUD-UAR	JOR-SAU
IRE-UNK	RUM-USR	CYP-GRC	VTN-CHN	JOR-UAR	UAR-YEM
CAN-USA	BOL-USR	UNK-GRC	SAF-RHO	YEM-UAR	CAM-TAI
USA-CAN	YUG-USR	UNK-IRE	IRO-IOR	USR-YUG	IND-NEP
	ALG-USR	USR-GME	JOR-SYR	SAU-JOR	TAI-CAM

APPENDIX C

Distributional Characteristics of the 24 Foreign Policy Output Variables

Type of Act	Mean	Std. Dev.	Range	Skewness[a]	Kurtosis[b]
1. Yield	0.26	0.90	0– 9	5.87	43.23
2. Comment	0.57	1.54	0–20	7.15	73.85
3. Explain	0.68	1.68	0–16	4.71	28.82
4. Meet	1.18	3.22	0–36	6.80	60.96
5. Visit	1.74	2.68	0–20	3.11	12.60
6. Host	1.74	2.68	0–20	3.11	12.60
7. Approve	1.04	2.13	0–14	3.37	13.09
8. Promise	0.56	1.62	0–15	5.85	41.44
9. Grant	1.06	2.06	0–20	4.27	25.87
10. Reward	0.77	2.15	0–25	5.91	48.19
11. Sub-agreement	0.91	1.83	0–20	5.66	48.22
12. Agree to meet	0.95	1.99	0–21	5.24	41.58
13. Request	0.70	1.60	0–20	5.86	54.45
14. Offer	0.39	1.46	0–19	8.07	81.84
15. Urge	0.61	1.90	0–24	7.51	74.35
16. Reject	1.06	3.22	0–44	8.12	87.88
17. $\sqrt{Charge}$[c]	1.12	1.56	0–11.4	2.89	12.18
18. Protest	1.09	3.62	0–36	6.83	53.81
19. Deny	0.49	1.82	0–22	7.65	72.51
20. Issue warning	0.91	2.79	0–28	6.02	44.13
21. Threatening display	0.79	2.17	0–27	6.27	58.52
22. Reduce relationship	0.58	1.24	0–13	4.17	27.43
23. Expel-seize	0.60	1.59	0–20	5.73	52.88
24. $\sqrt{Force}$[c]	0.46	1.30	0–11.2	5.27	34.21

a. A skewed distribution is one in which a large number of extreme cases are on one side of the distribution curve. The coefficients may be interpreted thusly: when the result is a positive number, the distribution is skewed to the right, and conversely, a negative number means the distribution is skewed to the left; and moreover, the size of the score indicates distance from the mean, so that large numbers are farther from the mean than are low scores.

b. Kurtosis refers to the general peakedness of a distribution. Positive coefficients are indicative of a distribution which is more peaked in the middle than the normal distribution, and negative values indicate a flatter distribution. Again, the size of the coefficient indicates the degree of the peakedness.

c. Because the raw distribution of this variable is so deviant, with extreme outliers so affecting its distributional characteristics, the original scores were transformed into their own square root. The statistics in this table describe the transformed distribution.

CHARLES W. KEGLEY, JR. *received his undergraduate education at the School of International Service, The American University, and his doctoral degree from the International Relations Program at Syracuse University. His publications include coeditorship of* A Multi-Method Introduction to International Politics *and* After Vietnam: The Future of American Foreign Policy, *and he has authored* "The Pattern of Foreign Policy Interaction in Asia: A Quantitative Comparison," *and* "Assessing the Impact of Trends in the International System." *He has taught at the School of Foreign Service at Georgetown University, and is now a member of the faculty at the University of South Carolina.*